C000063128

PRAC...
SOCIAL WORK

Series Editor: Jo Campling

BASW

Editorial Advisory Board:
Robert Adams, Terry Bamford, Charles Barker,
Lena Dominelli, Malcolm Payne, Michael Preston-
Shoot, Daphne Statham and Jane Tunstill

Social work is at an important stage in its development. All professions must be responsive to changing social and economic conditions if they are to meet the needs of those they serve. This series focuses on sound practice and the specific contribution which social workers can make to the well-being of our society.

The British Association of Social Workers has always been conscious of its role in setting guidelines for practice and in seeking to raise professional standards. The conception of the Practical Social Work series arose from a survey of BASW members to discover where they, the practitioners in social work, felt there was the most need for new literature. The response was overwhelming and enthusiastic, and the result is a carefully planned, coherent series of books. The emphasis is firmly on practice set in a theoretical framework. The books will inform, stimulate and promote discussion, thus adding to the further development of skills and high professional standards. All the authors are practitioners and teachers of social work representing a wide variety of experience.

JO CAMPLING

A list of published titles in this series follows overleaf

PRACTICAL SOCIAL WORK

Social Work and Europe

Crescy Cannan,
Lynne Berry
and
Karen Lyons

MACMILLAN

First published 1992 by
THE MACMILLAN PRESS LTD
Houndmills, Basingstoke, Hampshire RG21 2XS and London
Companies and representatives throughout the world

ISBN 0–333–56631–9 hardcover
ISBN 0–333–56632–7 paperback

A catalogue record for this book is available
from the British Library

Printed in Hong Kong

Series Standing Order (Practical Social Work)

If you would like to receive future titles in this series as they are published, you can make use of our standing order facility. To place a standing order please contact your bookseller or, in case of difficulty, write to us at the address below with your name and address and the name of the series. Please state with which title you wish to begin your standing order. (If you live outside the UK we may not have the rights for your area, in which case we will forward your order to the publisher concerned.)

Standing Order Service, Macmillan Distribution Ltd, Houndmills, Basingstoke, Hampshire, RG21 2XS, England.

To our colleagues in Europe

Contents

Preface

The context of British social work has changed dramatically over the last decade: citizens' and consumers' charters, choice and user involvement, and a rapid move to a more plural system, have reshaped the ideological and organisational field of social work. Old views on social work and its place in the welfare state have been shaken, especially by the reconstruction of community care services, by critiques of social workers' effectiveness in child protection, and by user groups who have challenged professional dominance in access to the provision of services. The 1989 Children Act, the 1990 NHS and Community Care Act and the 1991 Criminal Justice Act have transformed the framework and tasks of social work in the 1990s.

It has seemed to us, over a decade of visits to and contact with social work colleagues in other European countries, that we have much to learn from the different systems of welfare and the varied approaches of their social workers. This book aims to introduce readers to some continental European branches, traditions and organisational systems of social work, and to look at some examples which we have found encouraging during a time of disorientation and pessimism in the United Kingdom. We have stressed participative approaches and social action, and we have presented them in the context of the developing European Community and its goal of a Social Europe – which sanctions a social action role for social work.

We are aware of contradictory impulses in the EC and its member states. On the one hand we find moves to prevent marginalisation and exclusion, to promote human and social rights and to tackle all forms of discrimination. Yet we also see new nationalism in Eastern and Central Europe, and increasing racism and xenophobia within member states, trends which the liberalised internal market may exacerbate. We do not therefore consider 'Europe' an unequivocal blessing, but we do seek to enrich British social work with some of the optimism and strength that we have found elsewhere, especially in social action, which EC programmes encourage.

This book is a collective effort in that it grew from meetings of the authors over three years. However, prime responsibility for the chapters is as follows; Crescey Cannan 1, 2, 5; Lynne Berry 6, 7; and Karen Lyons 3 and 4. While the book is a shared responsibility, there are many colleagues in the fields of social work practice and education whom we would like to thank for their time, generosity and hospitality, in particular those listed in the acknowledgements.

CRESCEY CANNAN
LYNNE BERRY
KAREN LYONS

Acknowledgements

The authors would like to mention the help given by the following:

Lady Allen of Hartwood Memorial Trust – funding for Crescey Cannan's fieldwork in France.
Evi Despotide, Greek Association of Social Workers
Gunter Friesenhahn, Fachhochschule Rheinland Pfalz
Elinor Goldschmied, Freelance Consultant, London
Bernard Hall, CETTSW, London
Jytta Rhode Hanson, Danish social worker
Beresford Heywood, Adviser, EC, Paris
Sonia Jackson, University of Bristol
Didier Le Gall, Université de Caen
M. Le Masson, Caisse d'Allocations Familiales, Caen
Walter Lorenz, University of Cork
Christos Monzakitis, Greek Association of Social Workers
Elana Peláez, Spanish Association of Social Workers
Policy Officers, DG5, EC, Brussels
Laura Carli Sardi, University of Siena
Fredriech Seibel, European Centre for Community Education, Koblenz
Monika Simmel-Joachim, Fachhochschule Wiesbaden
Staff at VAMV, Frankfurt
Social Policy staff at DPVM, Frankfurt
Petros Stathopoulos, TEI, Athens
Amelia Tassmari Fissori, University of Turin
Nicole van Overbeek, Dutch Association of Social Workers
Eilis Walsh, Irish Association of Social Workers
Uwe Zeibarth, German Association of Social Workers

1

Social Europe: The Vision

Introduction: the context and aims of the book

The European Community (EC) is moving towards economic, and perhaps social and political, union. Already economic policies have had an impact on the world within which social work is practised. Policies of mobility of labour and capital have implications for families, individuals and communities. Student exchanges through the ERASMUS scheme are Europeanising higher education, including social work courses. The 1988 directive on the free movement of professionals, which came into force in 1991, will speed up the process of recognition of professional qualifications in EC countries and affect the length, level and content of training courses. Most local authorities have sections dealing with 'Europe', and many deprived areas receive funding from the EC.

These social and economic *policies* will have an effect on the context, framework and thinking of social work. There are also common social *trends* in Western Europe (for example, falling birth rates, youth unemployment, migration, increasing longevity, an increase in the number of lone parents, child abuse, and some urban and regional decline) which mean that social workers have similar clienteles and face similar challenges. Changes in East and Central Europe have added to a sense that a major restructuring of Europe is taking place at economic, social and cultural levels. These changes mean that this is an opportune time for social work to take stock of its outlook, training, values and practices, and to develop a European outlook to counterbalance the former reliance on Anglo-American theories and methods of intervention.

1

The book has two broad aims: first, to place British social work* in the framework of 'social Europe' and to identify some of the emerging European (supra-national) issues, policies and trends. While legislative and political detail are discussed, it is with *attitudes* that we shall be more concerned: with ways of thinking about the task of social work and of its relationship with its users. Second, we aim to draw some lessons from other European countries for social work in the UK; to give some pictures of social work practice in areas of France and Germany and, drawing on the thinking and practice of social workers and planners in a range of states, to make some suggestions as to the directions social work might take in the 1990s.

The book is based substantially, but not exclusively, on material derived from the authors' field visits to France and what used to be called West Germany. We will be selecting key themes which social workers, policy makers and planners have identified as important in their practice: the prevention of marginalisation and exclusion; the promotion of citizenship; social justice; participation; and user-involvement. This new thinking about 'the client' has grown in tandem with the reconceptualisation of the welfare states which were established across eastern and north-western Europe in the aftermath of the Second World War. Both right and left wingers have criticised such states, whether in terms of stigma, power of professions, cost, dependency or ineffectiveness in preventing poverty. The call for market systems, informal care or user-led systems of welfare has challenged received ideas as well as professional power and status. As social workers begin to work in partnership with a variety of groups and organisations they need to develop their thinking on accountability, user-involvement, and on future models of social protection. In the UK, new proposals for community care relying on care management have raised issues about the boundaries of social work, and the new patterns of training in the Diploma in Social Work have reintroduced

---

* We are aware of the differences in organisation and tradition between English and Scottish social work, but for convenience will mainly use the terms 'British social work' and 'social work in the UK.'

specialism after twenty years of genericism in training and practice. The 1980s were a decade of restrictions on social work and on its local government setting. The policing role of social work was emphasised, and social workers' experience of their work was dominated by crisis rather than prevention. Despite the interest in community social work at the start of that decade, it is the more 'technological' aspects of social work which are to the fore at the start of the 1990s, such as care management and procedures for assessing families and protecting children. These are important in that they may promote a practice characterised by greater clarity than has been the case, but there has been a loss of a broader role for social work, whether in preventive work with children and families, young people or community groups.

So social work in the UK is changing, and we would like to see this as a time to be open to ideas as to the directions and attitudes social work might choose. We shall not be looking at all fields and methods of social work or at training, but will tend to concentrate on social action and preventive/participative approaches, both because these are strong in the countries we shall look at and because this aspect of social work has suffered in the last decade in the UK. We hope we have not fallen into the trap of being naively overenthusiastic about social work in other countries (indeed, one of the benefits of visits abroad is that some of the strengths of the British system become clear). Other member states suffer from familiar problems of poverty, racism and urban stress. We know of criticisms of their social services and of their social workers. We are aware of having selected examples of good practice and of positive social thinking: we have done so deliberately in order to develop the theory and practice of social work in the UK.

The vision of social Europe

The vision of social Europe has its origins in debates on the nature and future of Western European nations in the aftermath of the Second World War; it is a vision which is becoming more intense because of its connection with the goal of economic and political union and with the arrival of the single market at the end of 1992. Those who have promoted this vision have argued that social Europe must be the twin of economic Europe: that a European social policy is crucial to economic development and also to minimise the inevitable costs of restructuring. As we shall show, there is an increasingly powerful voice which argues that social Europe is a goal in its own right. It is the embodiment of the values of social justice and democracy, not just the corrective or legitimating factor to economic policy. There are many statements of these goals; the one that follows is drawn from a document on the EC and Human Rights:

> The construction of Europe is not solely a matter of economics. Beyond the pragmatism of the Community's common policies – the fruits of history, necessity and will – human rights and fundamental freedoms are part of the common heritage of Europeans. With other concerns, such as education or culture they can stimulate our vision of the place of Europe in the world and the European model of society: a society in which individuals can thrive while being conscious of their obligations towards others – a unique model which we must all enrich and fulfill. (EC 5/89d, p. 10)

Jacques Delors, as President of the Commission of the European Communities since 1984, has furthered this vision. In his preface to the Cecchini Report (1988), which he entitled 'A Common Objective', he said that:

> [The EC] . . . has a social as well as an economic dimension, and must lead to a more unified Community. The twelve Member States have rightly decided that it should be accompanied by policies that will lead to greater unity as well as more prosperity. They have therefore strengthened Community technology policies and enlarged the resources available for helping the long-term unemployed, youth unemployment and rural development, as well as the backward regions of the Community and those facing major restructuring problems.
>
> This large market we are creating is of direct concern to every citizen of Europe. It is revolutionary, but it will be achieved both

because it is absolutely necessary and because it carries with it the goal of a united and strong Europe. (In P. Cecchini, 1988, p. xi)

The concern with unity, with solidarity, is central to this 'nation-building' process, and, as we shall see, it is a goal which impinges on the present and future tasks of social work. The twin halves of this concern are, first, to create a strong European identity which will be conducive to European economic growth (and to enhancing the place of Europe in the world), and second, to ensure social protection for those excluded or at risk of such exclusion in the process of economic change. Thus Delors has argued that the social dimension is essential to the deepening of the internal market and 'consists of, in its three forms: solidarity, pure and simple, the defence of the moral and material interests of the workers and, a minimum of agreement and participation in decision-making' (Delors, 1985, pp. xvii–xviii).

Many British people are under the impression that the EC represents a loss of sovereignty, a new layer of regulation, and a harmonisation of laws and social provision. We hope to show that this is not a helpful interpretation of Europeanisation, for it not only fails to grasp the progressive impact of EC principles on domestic social policy but it also prevents us making our own imaginative contribution to the European identity, and from participating in the social dialogue as to how European policies will be implemented in our own member states. We can analyse EC politics as a struggle between the proponents of social protection (reaching back into a long history of European social teaching) and those who advocate deregulation and liberation from 'interference' by the state in citizens' private lives. It is this tension in social philosophies which in 1990, came to a head over the UK's resistance to the 'Social Charter' (the Community Charter of the Fundamental Social Rights of Workers, Commission of the EC 1990b): the Thatcherite right presented this as an interference in national sovereignty and as too expensive for business. Other Conservatives and the Labour Party do not agree. In July 1990 Leon Brittan, the EC Commissioner and former Cabinet minister, attacked his fellow Conservatives for caricaturing the Community, for 'the British propensity for confusing regulation with interference' and thus the 'danger of being ignored at a critical and exciting phase of Europe's history' (quoted in *The Guardian*, 20 July 1990). This is a tension in social philosophies which we shall examine further in Chapter 2 and refer to in subsequent chapters. First, however, the origins and contemporary direction of the EC will set the scene.

The origins and structure of the EC

The foundation of the EC lies in the *Treaty of Rome*, which in 1957 established a common market with the goal of customs union and the elimination of tariff barriers between six European countries (France, West Germany, Italy and the Benelux countries). The Treaty spelt out its narrow objective of customs union, but included in its preamble a statement in which the social objectives 'appear . . . as absolutely predominant, like the lighthouse guiding the efforts of the economic and political union' (Rifflet, 1985, p. 19). These objectives included 'an ever closer union among the peoples of Europe', economic and social progress by common action, and the constant improvement of living and working conditions. It implied that economic union was a route to further political and social union in Europe (Rifflet, 1985, p. 20).

This narrow aim of customs union emerged out of as yet frustrated hopes which many Europeans held after the war for a framework of peaceful political cooperation, for a United States of Europe which would counterbalance the dangers of nationalism. The 'European movement' led to the establishment of the *Council of Europe* in 1949, to which 15 nations were affiliated. Its powers were reduced by the UK's reluctance to participate (Brewster and Teague, 1989). The 1951 Paris Treaty, signed by the six who would sign the Treaty of Rome, created the European Coal and Steel Community: a common European body regulating the industries needed to sustain war. These six countries wanted greater cooperation on defence, leading to the formation of the Western European Union in 1954. The Paris Treaty had been preceded by the Schuman Declaration in 1950:

> Europe will not evolve at a stroke, nor through an overall strategy; it will evolve through concrete achievements establishing firstly a factual solidarity. The bringing together of steel and coal production will ensure the immediate establishment of a *common base for economic development, the first stage towards a European Federation*. . . . this proposal will bring about the *first concrete foundations of European Federation which is indispensible to the preservation of peace.* (quoted in Rifflet, 1985, p. 18; italics in Rifflet)

The Council of Europe was to be important in developing concepts of human and social rights. In 1950 *The European Convention on Human Rights and Fundamental Freedoms* was drawn up, with contracting states' adherence to these rights to be supervised by the *European Court of Human Rights*. The Convention does not guarantee minimum levels of aid or state obligations towards citizens; on the contrary, it seeks to free citizens from state interference and requires respect for privacy (a stance understandable in the aftermath of Fascism). The Convention allows interference by public authorities only where rights or freedoms, or the health or morals of others should be protected. Consequently, the main body of cases brought to the Court at Strasbourg where social authorities have been involved are where there has been control or direct interference in private life (Hillestad Thune, 1987).

The European Social Charter (1961) was to introduce a more positive notion of rights and to broaden the field to social, economic and cultural rights. Here rights are conceived not as freedoms from state interference but as a set of reciprocal obligations between citizen and state. It gives a clear statement of the right to work, to form a trade union, to vocational training, to health care, to social security and to social assistance (rights which echo older constitutions, such as the 1971 French Constitution with its right to work, and the United Nations Declaration of 1949). Furthermore, children and young persons and the institution of the family have the right to social protection. The right of migrant workers and their families to protection and assistance is stated.

Contracting (Council of Europe) states did not have to sign all the articles and the fact that the Charter did not lay down minimum standards meant that it could not demand the adoption of new levels of social protection. Its force, however, was in the new attitudes it enshrined: an emphasis on human dignity, on 'want' rather than poverty, and a stress that persons receiving social and medical assistance should not suffer from a diminution of political and social rights. The new post-war welfare states should not reduce those who could not support themselves to the status of second-class citizens, as had been the case in the days of charity and the Poor Law. Assistance was a right, and not just a subjective right but an obligation on the part of contracting parties to provide such assistance. The Charter also introduced the notion of decency thresholds, and the right of workers to a decent standard of living. It emphasised assistance but stressed the elimination of want as the ultimate goal, echoing the Beveridge Report, but also anticipating new ways of tackling social problems and the need for coordinated social action in the fulfilment of social objectives (Mayer Fabian, 1987, pp. 27–33).

We will return to the impact on Britain of the European Convention and of the European Court of Human Rights in Chapters 6 and 7. Here we need to note that the *Single European Act* of 1986 (which completed the Treaty of Rome and committed member states to economic union by the end of 1992) mentions in its Preamble both the European Convention on Human Rights and the European Social Charter. These are described as the cornerstones for the construction of Europe. But what is the structure of the EC itself, and how are its policies implemented?

The key political institutions of the European Community are

the European Commission (Brussels)
the European Parliament (Strasbourg/Luxembourg)
the Council of Ministers (Brussels)
the European Court of Justice (Luxembourg)

The European Commission is the EC Civil Service, but it is also the body that proposes and follows through laws. There are 17 Commissioners, nominated by national governments, including Delors as President. The Commission comprises 23 Directorates-General, of which DG5 – Employment, Industrial Relations and Social Affairs – is of most interest and relevance to social work.

The European Parliament has 518 MEPs, 81 from the UK. The largest political grouping is the Socialists, followed by the (conservative) Christian Democrats. As yet the Parliament does not directly legislate: its role is consultative and advisory. The Council of Ministers is the final decision-making body. It consists of government ministers from each member state. EC law consists of *Regulations* (which immediately apply to member states regardless of national law), and *Directives* (which are introduced by the European Commission, and decided upon by the Council of Ministers). They are adopted (and adapted) into national law by member states.

The European Court of Justice (which must not be confused with the European Court of Human Rights, the Council of Europe Court which has only moral status) consists of 13 judges, one from each member state, and one rotating. Judgements on legal disputes overrule national courts, but the court has no sanctions if member states ignore judgements (*Which?*, 1991).

An example of the working of the EC is seen in the field of equal opportunities. In 1975 the Commission issued an Equal Pay Directive, requiring member states to take measures to ensure that the principle of equal pay for work of equal value was applied. In 1976 the Equal Treatment Directive was issued. This outlawed discrimination on grounds of sex, directly or indirectly, by reference to family and marital status, in access to employment, promotion, working conditions and vocational training. It required governments to set up the means for individuals to pursue claims, and it stipulated that states should take measures to ensure that employees were protected from dismissal as a consequence of complaints or of the enforcement of the principle of equal treatment. In 1978 the Social Security Directive extended the principle of equal opportunities to include statutory social security schemes, and this was extended to private sector schemes in 1986. In 1983 draft directives were issued on leave for family reasons up to two years after birth, with more generous leave for parents of children with special needs or for single parents. Employees would also be entitled to leave for family reasons, such as the death of a spouse or near relative, or the wedding of a child. These draft directives have not been ratified by the Council as a result of opposition from some governments, notably the UK.

The European Court of Justice has monitored and furthered equal opportunities legislation, and has dealt with more cases from the UK than from any other EC country (Brewster and Teague, 1989). In 1984 the Court ruled that the UK did not given sufficiently clear rights to women to claim equal pay for work of equal value: while the government amended the Equal Pay Act of 1970, the British Equal Opportunities Commission is still not satisfied that the amendments reflect the Court's decision. In 1986 the Court ruled that the UK was unlawful in making women retire before men. A significant ruling was that concerning Invalid Care Allowance from which married women had been barred: the Court ruled that married women should not be treated differently from men or single women.

The development of EC social policies

Brewster and Teague (1989) delineate three phases in the development of EC social policy. The *first phase* was from 1957 to 1972; the emphasis was on increasing labour mobility inside the Common Market, and action consisted of legalistic measures in reducing barriers to the free movement of workers. This phase saw the floating of ideas on wider social intervention with some modest beginnings in the fields of equal opportunities, health and safety, social security for workers moving between member states, the establishment of the Social Fund, and of initiatives on youth. But progress was slow and to some extent taken up by negotiations over the entry of the UK, Denmark and Ireland. The resignation of de Gaulle and the election of Pompidou to the Presidency of France in 1969 brought a new optimism. In 1969 member states affirmed their commitment to the political objective of a United States of Europe, the aim of economic and monetary union, and the enlargement of the Community. In 1972 the Summit members instructed the Commission and other Community bodies to start immediate work on monetary union and on the development of a range of policies in the social field. In the same year Britain, Denmark and Ireland signed the accession treaties for entry the following year. An interventionist policy was developing, connecting economic with social development.

What motivated the member states to develop the nature and direction of social policy? One reason may have been the worsening economic conditions from the early 1970s, with growing unemployment and monetary upheavals. Another reason was ideological: the calling into question, especially by the student movement, of the principle of economic growth at any price. Leaders like Willi Brandt had called attention to regional disparities, to the North–South divide, and to growing differences between sectors of the European population; Brandt called for a 'human face' to the integration endeavour. There was a general concern about inequalities in the face of abundance: a 'rediscovery of poverty'. The accession of the UK, Denmark and Ireland had brought new civil servants to Brussels, keen to widen the scope of social affairs beyond employment policy. Member states became more active in setting a common policy agenda, formalising their meetings in the summits now known as the European Council.

These attitudes ushered in the *second phase*, from 1972 to 1983. This was a more positive and interventionist phase, with calls for a more equitable and socially just European society, and for more social integration as well as for the harmonisation and progressive upgrading of standards in employment practices and in the labour market. The Irish Fine Gael–Labour coalition government, newly elected, was keen to put together a new social policy and to be seen to be tackling the problem of poverty without necessarily overcommitting themselves, especially given the curbs on

expenditure following the 1973–4 oil crisis. The Irish proposal of pilot poverty programmes found their way into both
EC and Irish policies: 'It could show the "human face" of
Europe without specific policy commitments and within budgetary limits acceptable to the Council of Ministers,' (Dennett
et al., 1982, p. 4).

At the Paris Summit in 1972 the Heads of Government of
the member states committed themselves to action in the
social field stating that social action is as important as economic union, and a necessary step towards that goal. Accordingly a Social Action Programme was announced the following year for the years 1974–6. The programme enshrined
three broad principles which should guide Community action in the social field:

1. full and better employment;
2. improvement of living and working conditions;
3. greater participation in the economic and social decisions of the Community by workers and management.

The plan mentions action for migrant workers of member
states or third countries, action to achieve equality between
men and women in work and training, action on health and
safety, action for handicapped workers, and the launching of
pilot schemes to combat poverty. (The poverty programmes
will be discussed later in this chapter.)

The *third phase* dates from the early 1980s. The profile and
legitimacy of the EC was raised with the first direct elections
to the European Parliament in 1979, yet the EC remained
highly bureaucratic and with an ineffective decision-making
process. The work of some MEPs gradually forced a change:
Altiero Spinelli and other MEPs created a working group in
1981 on the future of the EC. This group's work led to the
Single European Act of 1986 which was to commit the member states to a liberalised internal market by the end of 1992,
along with a commitment to social protection and measures
to strengthen economic and social cohesion and the creation of a stronger common political role for the Community.
This move was strongly supported by President Mitterrand of
France.

Jacques Delors has provided much of the vision during this period of determination to make union a going concern and more than just a free trade zone. His quandary was that, if the Commission tried to establish a social dimension to the Community by the legislative route, it ran the risk of being accused of forcing change against national patterns. On the other hand, if no Community legislation existed the result would be that EC social policy would be nothing more than a series of non-binding guidelines (Brewster and Teague, 1989, pp. 94–6). As a way forward Delors promoted the concept, originally floated by the French government in 1981, of *l'espace social* (literally, the social space). The completion of the internal market by the end of 1992 was to be accompanied by a framework of social partnership between employers and trade unions whose dialogue, he hoped, would create the broad ideas for EC policies. This social framework was seen as necessary in the control of processes of 'social dumping' (a competitive devaluation of wages and deregulation of employment conditions in order to keep or attract capital). So what we see in this concept, at the heart of the third phase, is a withdrawal from the aim of harmonisation of provision and laws, to a new means of negotiating and creating broad principles which would be implemented in ways that suited individual member states. At the same time European citizenship and culture, and social measures to prevent exclusion and to provide safety nets of social protection, are promoted. In this view the societal aspect is an essential, not optional, element. Vandamme (1985) and Rifflet (1985) have distinguished the social (that is, social protection policies) from the societal policies which are those concerned with the 'big' aims of European union, identity and personality.

The process is not smooth: the dialogue between 'the social partners' has disappointed Delors (speech to TUC Congress, 1988) and the Commission has taken a lead in setting the policy agenda. There are conflicts between the majority of the member states who wish to see a Community committed to social protection, and those (dominated by the UK) who want a Community limited to economic deregulation, with the Social Fund concentrating on supporting small

and medium-sized businesses. The UK Conservative government of the 1980s under Mrs Thatcher saw the social dimension of the EC as restricted to the creation of jobs and the
reduction of unemployment, viewing employment contracts
as private matters between employers and their staff: a
policy reflected in the reduction of employment protection
and rights in British legislation since 1979 (Wedderburn,
1990).

In 1990 the conflict between the social protectionists and
the deregulationists centred on the *Community Charter of Fundamental Social Rights of Workers*: the 'Social Charter'. The
Charter was adopted by 11 of the 12 member states in 1989
and, as indicated above, represents the culmination, with the
action programme for implementing the charter, of the
Commission's decision to push ahead with the implementation of the internal market. Delors, in his speeches to the
TUC and to the European Trade Union Confederation in
1988, argued that the internal economic market must also be
designed to benefit each and every citizen of the Community, and that the social dimension of the European construction must include social rights of workers (including
those of training and participation in management).

The charter, in accordance with the subsidiarity principle
(see Chapter 2), places a responsibility on member states *'in
accordance with national practices'* to guarantee rights which
include protection for part-time and temporary workers, for
pregnant women, health and safety, rights to 'decent' wages
and 'minimum incomes', and worker participation in com-
pany management; it also states the necessity for measures to
combat discrimination in every form. The Commission will
issue directives contained in its action programme of social
legislation, and member states will be expected to ensure
that their legislation, takes account of the minimum standards enshrined in the charter. As Wedderburn points out,
there is an ambiguity about whether the social dimension
comprises measures which are part of the economic market
– the welfare to make competition work – 'Or does it go
further and include measures of social justice and priorities
based on human need which may take precedence even over

the bottom line of the accountants' judgements on efficiency?'
(Wedderburn, 1990, p. 9).

What is notable about the third and contemporary phase
is the return to the big issue of creating the European space,
the European citizen, the societal rather than merely social
issues. Economic problems since the 1973–4 oil crisis, and
the growth of social security and health care budgets as
proportions of national GDPs, have prompted governments
either to cut back expenditure *per se*, or to find new ways of
meeting social needs. EC policy, which strongly reflects French
policy under Mitterrand, has during the 1980s recognised
that social policy can no longer be conceived only as a corrective to economic policy and performance, but is itself a
crucial part of meeting the challenge of rising unemployment and slowing growth. The current tasks of social policy
then are, first, to find new ways of meeting needs, and second, to act on society in ways which can promote growth and
employment. EC and French social policy is concerned with
facing the fact that the welfare state is in some ways out-
moded and unpopular. It is therefore a move from Keynes
and Beveridge to something new which is seen as necessary
to economic revival. It means including education and the
environment in social policy, alongside new patterns of work
(such as cooperatives and work-sharing) and of cultural action to promote solidarity and participation (Vandamme,
1985). Jean-Pierre Cot, the French leader of the (dominant)
Socialist group at the European Parliament, argued at the
1989 Labour Party conference that modern social democracy has four main components: a form of economic
liberalism, a high degree of social protection, human and
democratic rights, and a certain cultural identity. There is an
acknowledged pragmatism in looking for ways of making
economic efficiency compatible with social protection. He
argues that this project is only partly a response to
Thatcherism: it was in the difficulties of Callaghan's policies
that the limitations of the traditional welfare state became
evident (*The Guardian*, 17 November 1989). Because it is
about changing the post-war social welfare framework, the
European project directly concerns social work. We shall

now go on to look briefly at the major EC social programmes, their philosphies and methods.

EC social policies: from exclusion to equal opportunities

We need to assess EC social policy in two ways: (a) the ways in which EC directives and rulings have affected member states' legislation and have set standards against which groups pressing for change can set their demands; and (b) the ideological impact of the action programmes' methods of intervention and statements of social rights, citizenship and so forth. The former will be discussed in Chapter 6; the latter is the concern of the rest of this chapter.

Hoskyns (1985) has documented the initiatives for women in the Social Affairs Directorate from the early 70s. The incoming Irish Commissioner and British civil servants wished to expand social policies beyond employment policies. Jacqueline Nonon, the Frenchwoman in charge of women's policy, worked hard to shift policy from formal to substantive measures, getting these adopted in the Social Action Plan of 1973. This stated that priority should be given to facilities to enable women to reconcile family responsibilities with job aspirations. However, the two Directives on equal pay and equal treatment were much more cautious: positive measures were now only mentioned in a permissive sense, and the scope of the legislation was once again limited to formal equality:

> The gradual down-playing of the issue of family responsibilities in the whole question of . . . women in the labour market was partly due to a genuine doubt about Community competence [in the fields of family policy], but also the gradual imposition of the patriarchal view . . . [by] the Commission/Council hierarchy. (Hoskyns, 1985, p. 84).

This story illustrates EC reluctance during the second phase to promote special treatment: without pressure Commission policy reverts to a 'workerist' employment policy; with pressure it broadens to include the social as well as the economic aims of the Treaty of Rome. In the field of women's policy such pressure has been notable, partly because the Directives *have* had an impact on states (they have set up monitoring and grievance mechanisms and they have set standards on which to campaign); but also because women's organisations have been effective in exchanging information, both autonomously and at semi-official levels (as with the European Network of Women, based in Brussels; see Chapter 6).

As a result, in the early 1980s the Commission moved on from legislation which merely freed women to compete with men, to the promotion of equal opportunities via special treatment programmes and measures. A first Action Programme was adopted in 1981. At this point migrant women emerged as a key group requiring Community support, and it was recognised that disadvantage rather than citizenship needed to be a criterion (Prondzynski, 1989, p. 348). The priority of migrant women was reiterated in the Medium Term Action Programme on Equal Opportunities for Women (1986–90). In 1987 the European Parliament called for action to improve the situation of all migrant women at both EC and national levels, recognising their particular vulnerability in the face of economic restructuring (this will be further discussed in chapter 2).

To some extent this recognition had grown from the priority women had in the European Social Fund (ESF), whose focus is job creation, often in small-scale local initiatives or self-employment schemes, and training, with the main aims of combating long-term unemployment and integrating young people into working life. In the past the ESF has supported schemes run by and for women (in 1985 the share of women in the overall volume of aid provided by the Fund was 38 per cent; the number of women receiving aid was approximately one million, with the UK receiving 31 per cent of the total sum spent on women (see Commission of the EC, 1987b, cited in Whitting and Quinn, 1989, p. 338).

However, recently the ESF has dropped women as one of its main priorities. ESF activities will be targeted on the long-term unemployed and young people up to 25. It is recognised that women, disabled people and migrant workers will experience particular difficulties in entering the formal labour market, and are therefore vulnerable to segregation in less favoured sectors. There is, however, a programme promoting equal opportunities for women in the fields of employment and vocational training (NOW) which will be implemented in the context of the third programme for equal opportunities. There is a parallel programme for handicapped persons (HORIZON) which will reinforce the HELIOS programme on disability (Commission of the EC, 1990c), which was the result of the Commission report in 1986 on the Employment of Disabled People. This had announced an Action Programme to promote the social integration of disabled people by the harmonisation and progressive raising of standards in each member state. NOW and HORIZON aim to enable women and disabled people to participate fully in labour markets by making vocational training more effective. NOW will support child-care facilities as a necessary complementary measure; HORIZON will support adaptations to the workplace, and the rehabilitative, social and counselling help which disabled people might need in entering the labour market (Social Europe, 2/1989). IRIS, launched in 1988, is a network of vocational training programmes for women, again designed to prevent labour market segregation. The issue of child-care provision is of course central in the promotion or denial of equal opportunity, as demonstrated by the EC Child Care Network Report (Moss, 1988), which recommended that the Community take major initiatives to improve the situation in child-care services. (These initiatives will be further discussed in Chapter 6.)

The right of migrants within the EC to social security and employment protection has been a concern in all EC treaties. In 1974 action was proposed to ensure that migrants are covered by member states' social security and pension schemes, to promote better information and training for staff of public agencies in contact with migrants, to improve the quality of legal assistance and representation, and the use of the Social Fund to sponsor training projects for migrants. There was a Directive on the Education of Children of Migrant Workers in 1977 which was concerned with the children of migrant workers from other member states, and required that host member states should 'promote the teaching of the mother tongue and of the culture of the country of origin of the above mentioned children'. This arose from a resolution in 1976 on the priority of education for migrant workers and their families; it is concerned with the movement of EC nationals and not primarily with minorities. However, a statement extended the applicability of the Directive to children of nationals of non-member countries, so that ethnic minorities and Third World immigrants were also covered.

More recently racism and xenophobia have become a focus. An all-party group of MEPs chaired by Glyn Ford, the Labour Group leader at Strasbourg, produced a report in 1990 with recommendations for harmonising Community laws on discrimination and improving the monitoring of racism, anti-Semitism and the activities of the extreme right. Recommendations include a directive to outlaw discrimination, the giving of voting rights to immigrants in local elections, a charter of rights for residents of Community countries, sanctions against employers who exploit illegal immigrants, and the use of EC funds in developing education to improve understanding of cultural differences (*The Guardian*, 24 July 1990). While the Social Affairs Commissioner, Vasso Papandreou, was keen to develop a common EC initiative, there was doubt that the UK would wish to welcome a further charter of rights (*The Independent*, 28 September 1990), despite the fact that many of the recommendations reflect a British report by the Runnymede Trust (1987) on racism and xenophobia in the EC. We shall further discuss the positions of women and minorities in Chapter 2, and in Chapter 6 we shall look at the impact of the EC initiatives described here.

The poverty programmes

At the time of writing we are at the start of the third EC poverty programme (whose title no longer contains the word poverty due to reluctance by the German and British governments to acknowledge its existence). These action programmes are important to social workers because they are in the tradition of community work/development/action which is currently 'unfashionable' in the UK, but which is actively promoted in these programmes. They emphasise the participation of the populations involved, and they espouse a social structural view of poverty which can be contrasted to a tendency in the new right (and sometimes in the casework/ therapeutic tradition in contemporary social work) to individualise problems and to blame the victim. The first poverty programme was approved by the Commission in 1975, having had its gestation in the concern to give the community a 'human face' (Dennett *et al.*, 1982). The programme consisted originally of 21 schemes and studies over two years. Pressure from the German projects extended this to five. There were three elements: the projects themselves funded 50–50 with national governments; an evaluative study of the projects; and studies on the nature and extent of poverty in individual member states. The definition of poverty used by the Council in 1975 is descended from Townsend's 'persons beset by poverty: individuals or families whose resources are so small as to exclude them from the minimum acceptable way of life of the Member State in which they live' (quoted in Dennett *et al.*, 1982, p. 155).

The main method of the poverty programmes was to be (in a wide sense) community work. The *Aide à Toute Détresse* movement (which ran six of the projects in the programme) had, according to Dennett *et al.*, the most clearly articulated theory of a victim group, 'which it termed the Fourth World to symbolise its exclusion from the rest of affluent western society. The Fourth World is the sub-proletariat, the people who exist on the fringes of the labour market excluded from the main structures of economic, political and social life' (Dennett *et al.*, 1982 p. 201). This approach meant a solidarity with the poor, which went hand in hand with the requirement that the projects involved the populations concerned in both planning and running the projects. The second main requirement was that the projects should be innovative: it was hoped that through their practice and collaboration with other projects in other member states, states would develop their own strategies and understanding of poverty.

The clear evidence of continuing and of new poverty meant that in 1984 the Council of Ministers acknowledged the need for further action. This second poverty programme was directed at 'the Fourth World', the new poor, as much as at those in 'traditional' poverty (we shall examine the debates on the 'new poverty' in Chapter 2). Now the Commission declared its clear involvement in the fight against poverty, placing the poverty programme next to its partners, the Social Fund (implementing training and job creation), regional policy which develops disadvantaged areas, and other actions (such as the fight against illiteracy). The Commission stated that:

> The persistence of poverty or even of a precarious work situation is incompatible with several key objectives of the European Treaties: to promote a harmonized development of economic activity throughout the Community, continuous and balanced expansion, increase stability, and an accelerated improvement in living standards. A people's Europe should be a Europe of solidarity, especially as regards the most underprivileged. (Commission of the EC, 1987b)

Accordingly the second programme was launched to cover the period 1985–8, with similar objectives to the first programme (although now larger in scope, with 65 projects and a stronger emphasis on dissemination of results to all those engaged in combating poverty, especially local authorities and social workers). The projects focused on disadvantaged urban districts, impoverished rural areas, single-parent families, second-generation migrants, refugees, returning migrants, and on homeless, marginal, elderly and unemployed people.

The third poverty programme was launched in 1989. The Commission (Commission of the EC, 1989c) pointed to the range of other measures to combat poverty in the EC (food aid measures, literacy schemes, employment creation). The programme reiterates the original approach (action-research projects, dissemination and exchange of knowledge, transfer of innovative methods). Now, however, the programme is more dominated by the aim of reinforcing social and economic cohesion in the Community and of finding innovative socio-cultural methods of doing so. Despite economic growth rates of around 3 per cent, proportions on social assistance appear to be rising in member states: the first poverty programme estimated that approximately 38 million people were in poverty in member states (income less than half the average per capitum income in their country), while the interim report on the second programme estimated 44 million in 1985.

The lessons drawn from the second programme were that the recognition of social and cultural exclusions in poverty transformed the methods used by traditional charity and social work organisations in the older member states, and that public and private organisations could work effectively together.

The Commission asserted that successful action must tackle every facet of poverty, and move beyond social assistance to measures to counteract the demoralisation and impotence of those trapped in poverty: the long-term unemployed, one-parent families, immigrants, elderly people and so on. Economic and social development of the project areas should be combined. It was planned that the programme would finance 30 pilot schemes, managed by a committee of representatives of all the bodies involved in carrying out the scheme, who would undertake to complete a joint programme to combat all facets of poverty in their region, province or town: 'Implementation of such a partnership (with the active participation of the representatives of the disadvantaged) will itself constitute a major innovation in the anti-poverty campaign' (ibid., p. 11).

The programme has gone on to develop the theme of the articulation between economic and social integration: projects are expected to identify a strategy of economic and social integration of less favoured groups. The philosophy is that merely giving the poor money will not tackle the issue of 'precariousness': the poor need the means to overcome their poverty, which include good housing, good health and food, medical care, education, urban renewal, and a healthy environment. Only when these are tackled together will the cycles of marginalisation and the reinforcement of exclusion be prevented.

This thinking draws much from French social policy during the 1980s (see Chapter 5). Socio-cultural support is combined with economic integration, and the project papers are littered with the words 'solidarity', 'social cohesion', 'integration' (*insertion*), 'multi-dimensional approach', 'revitalisation of neighbourhoods', 'combating exclusion'. The project profiles of the first pilot projects in what has now been named ELISE (European Information-Exchange Network on Local Development and Local Employment Initiatives) states:

> In underprivileged neighbourhoods throughout the European Community's twelve member states, innovative initiatives are being taken to bring them back to life. Bold policies are being implemented at national level, particularly in France . . .
>
> In particular, France has achieved much in this field, thanks to an interministerial policy for the social development of neighbourhoods, which was launched as early as 1982. (ELISE, 1989b)

One aspect of this programme which may have a direct impact on social work is the suggestion that a new professional is created: the social urban development agent, who will have the task of connecting economic and social development, and of animating the partners in a coordinated way (a view resisted at a European Liaison Meeting of the International Federation of Social Workers (IFSW) in April 1990).

Conclusion: an opportunity for social work?

In this chapter we have given an idea of the development of the vision of social Europe. It is clear that while there tends to be something of a consensus in European social thinking as to the need for social and societal policies, the centrality of a social dimension to the EC's (rather than member states') policies is debatable. In this sense there is not a single European social policy which will be imposed on member states; instead we are in a time of change, negotiation and creativity. Because the social policies are evolving, it seems to us crucial that social workers participate in promoting the social dimension of the EC, playing a part in widening the vision of what it could encompass and thus enriching both national and local policies. We have shown that much EC social policy is in reality employment policy to sort out snags in the free movement of labour or mop up the victims. But some initiatives are much wider, encompassing family support, the environment, positive action for women, disabled workers and ethnic minorities; they encompass the quality of life and not just the workplace. There is a vision in the EC initiatives and programmes that includes social work in wide-ranging social and community action, which not only recaptures something of a lost role of social work but offers new thinking on social intervention. We consider that many of the EC initiatives could get us away from 'clientism': we could see 'clients' more as workers (albeit in the most precarious sectors), as participants, and as citizens. We would like to see social Europe as central both to the European project and to the interests of the users of social services, not least because without this dimension the liberalised internal market may cost many of the more precariously placed groups dearly. We hope, therefore, that the following chapters will encourage readers to participate in the dialogue and creation of this vision.

The next chapter will look more closely at social policy in other member states, and at the social trends which provide the context of social work. This will enable us to move in subsequent chapters to look at the organisation and practice of social work in other member states, and to reflect on its relevance for social work in the UK.

2

Contexts of Social Work: Social Policies and Social Trends in Contemporary Europe

Introduction

This chapter will begin with a general background to the development of welfare states in Europe, and a look at the principles and philosophies of welfare which they enshrine. The ways in which they have converged, both in terms of social trends and in terms of social protection, will be discussed and set against some key differences between the British approach and those of other member states. In the main we shall be referring to the industrialised northern states, but we shall note the separate problems of the more agricultural southern states. Social trends (of poverty, migration and racism, and of family stress and change) will be considered in order to give a portrait of the population with which social work is concerned. The intention of this chapter, then, is to give a picture of the ideological and social context of social work in some European member states (especially France and what was 'West' Germany). We shall look at the principles underlying social policies in different states in order to consider the tasks of social work: we shall argue that where social solidarity is the key aim of social policies (rather than the relief of individual need), social work is more likely to have as its mandate the prevention of exclusion of groups and the promotion of participation and integration of the marginalised. The preventive, educative and community aspects of social work will be as much in evidence as the more individualistic approach familiar to English social workers.

Social policy, social work and welfare states: historical development

A striking difference between member states is that the term 'welfare state' is not one universally used or admired. The field of activities we are referring to and how we name it is problematic; even the term 'social policy' has a different connotation and history in different European countries (C. Jones, 1979). To some extent this is rooted in a different, continental social philosophy; specific historical and industrial conditions have also affected the development of welfare states, and of institutionalised systems of social protection.

The British term 'welfare state' made its way around the world after 1945. Beveridge, although the architect of the welfare state, did not like the term, whose usage had begun in 1941 as a contrast to the power and warfare state of the Nazis (Flora and Heidenheimer, 1984). Beveridge preferred the term social service state, considering the term 'welfare state' to have 'brave new world' connotations. Nevertheless, the term gained credence and, in the time of post-war reconstruction, the Beveridge model of the welfare state was diffused by British intellectuals (for instance, Peacock, Titmuss, and Beveridge himself) who toured the zones of Germany controlled by the Allies. The Beveridge report had already been disseminated as propaganda in occupied France by the Allies (Spicker, 1991), where it influenced the 1945 social welfare legislation (Thevenet and Desigaux, 1985).

The Beveridge model built on the democratic, collectivised conditions of war: the solidarity and sense of common purpose, and the extension of free medical care, nursery care, emergency housing and employment protection purely on the basis of need. What impressed the socialist parties and many voters in wartime Europe were the uniformity, clarity and range of the Beveridge proposals.

Yet, after the war, the German SPD (Social Democratic Party), like the conservative CDU (Christian Democrats), rejected the idea of a comprehensive health care system, preferring a decentralised plural system. Similarly they disliked the proposed flat rate benefits, preferring earnings-related benefits to encourage initiative and preserve status (Hockerts, 1981). When the British occupying forces in Germany tried to break the German social insurance principle whereby only the weakest were protected by the state (the majority insuring themselves through a multitude of private insurance funds) and introduce the Beveridge scheme of general social insurance for the whole nation, they were met with protest. The middle classes objected to the loss of choice if the different insurance funds were nationalised, and the trade unions protested at the low level of the proposed flat rate benefits, preferring the German system of status preservation.

German history and culture, then, provoked a different attitude to the Beveridge welfare state: 'In Britain the war experience had engendered a sense of national solidarity and confidence in state intervention and had thus prepared the ground for the Beveridge reforms; in Germany by contrast, the experience of Nazi misuse of power had provoked opposition to any, form of government imposed centralisation or collectivism, (Hockerts, 1981, pp. 317–18). The new CDU government in West Germany asserted its pride in the pre-Nazi German pioneering social insurance system instituted by Bismarck in the 1880s. Adenauer said, at a CDU rally in 1946: 'We must hold on to this social insurance. We are proud of it. And as for the proposals Beveridge has recently made in Hamburg, I can only say that we Germans have already had such things these past thirty years' (Hockerts, 1981, p. 318). This sentiment was shared by the SPD, and until the 1980s it was possible to speak of a consensus over the desirability of the German *Sozialstaat* (the social state), rather than the *Wohlfahrtsstaat* (the welfare state), which has negative, patronising connotations (Zapf, 1986).

So, while we find convergences in social welfare developments in Western European states, we also find divergencies in philosophy which arise out of both the culture and the specific experiences of those countries. This point is a particularly stark one in the current search for future models of welfare in Eastern Europe, given the unhappy experience of state provision: is there a way between the authoritarian, paternalistic state and the free market, a way which could retain a progressive vision of citizenship and social justice as articulated from below (Deacon and Szalai, 1991)? The real gain from comparative work is, then, a questioning of what we believe to be the 'right' kind of social services, and a fresh look at concepts like choice and self-help which tend to be treated with suspicion by British social workers who are less accustomed to a plural system.

There are similarities in the historical growth of the welfare states of the West (the USA and Japan are complex exceptions to many of the common trends). Social security and social insurance were first established in the 1880s in Bismarck's laws which attracted immense interest in other European countries. Denmark copied all three German pension schemes (old age, sickness and accident) between 1891 and 1898, Belgium between 1894 and 1903, and Britain from 1905 to 1911 (Briggs, 1961). Public education, housing, health and sanitation, and factory legislation were similarly burgeoning between the mid-nineteenth century and early twentieth century, with much interest in other countries' schemes. It was the common experience (albeit in different decades) of rapid industrialisation and urbanisation and the growth of the trade union movement which underlay such developments, although each nation's social policies developed according to its specific needs to develop the quality of its industrial and military force, as well as to respond to or control trade union demands and the growing power of social democracy once suffrage was extended to working-class men.

States' expenditure on social security has risen over the twentieth century and coverage extended from insured workers to their dependents and then to most of the population. Gough (1979) notes two main trends: (a) France and Germany and certain other European countries had early social insurance for certain occupational groups, and over the post-war period have gradually moved to national social minima and universal coverage (often through state-backed 'private' insurance funds); (b) Britain and Scandinavia established national minimum flat-rate benefits which were gradually augmented by earnings-related benefits. Both groups of countries were in much the same place by the end of the 1970s, the first group moving from benefits which preserved differences to a certain universalism, the second moving from an egalitarian flat-rate system to greater inequalities in earnings-related systems. Despite differences, then, the northern European countries have a moved from residual services (*laissez-faire*, limited to safety net) to institutional provision (comprehensive, state-backed social rights). Differences in the ways in which such services and benefits are delivered will be the concern of the section below on pluralism.

Personal social services have similar histories in northern European countries 'Locking up the poor' had been the public response to vagabondage from the sixteenth century onwards (for instance, in l'Hôpital Général in Paris). The Catholic church also developed charitable schemes for assisting the poor in the community, such as *les maisons de charité*, or the work of St. Vincent de Paul, and typically one finds that lay and church social provision continues to coexist on the continent (Rodgers *et al.*, 1979). The French infant life protection movement influenced that in England and the legislation of the 1870s (Behlmer, 1982), as did the infant welfare movement of the 1880s with its lady visitors and *consultations de nourrisons* (infant nutrition advice).

The first child protection legislation is found in 1889 in Britain and in France, in 1901 in the Netherlands, 1905 in Denmark, and 1912 in Belgium. These countries all moved from punitive attitudes to both parents and children to community- and treatment-based approaches run by social workers, within the framework of laws establishing juvenile courts and associated services such as placements for children or preventive help for mothers (in 1908 in Britain, 1912 in France and 1924 in Germany). The 1970s saw the growth of radical criticisms of social work, often from within social work, and movements to establish clearer parents' and children's rights (see Rood-de Boer, 1984, on the Netherlands). The same decade saw the 'discovery' of the battered baby influenced by Kempe's work, and the 1980s a concern with child sexual abuse. All the northern European countries have moved to develop treatment, reporting and monitoring of abusive families; and to a greater emphasis on multi-disciplinary team work (Davies and Sale, 1989). At the same time concern at media criticisms of social workers, blaming them for the deaths of children at risk, has been noted by social workers (see Meyer and Derrien, 1990, on France). Such criticism perhaps reflects a certain neotraditionalism in attitudes to parental responsibility, tied to new right criticisms of the welfare state (Hegar, 1989).

Social work has remarkably similar histories in northern European countries, emerging from charity visiting and organisation, from settlements, from work in institutions with children, public health, housing and factory welfare. Social workers in the nineteenth century had considerable influence on each other: for example, the English Charity Organisation Society modelled their casework principles on the German system of poor relief and visiting in Elberfeld (itself influenced by the earlier British system), on charitable visiting in Bavaria and Hamburg, and on the work of the society of St Vincent de Paul in France (Woodroofe, 1962, pp. 45–7). Settlements were of international interest: Jane Addams' work in the USA and the English settlements were known to Mlle Gaherty in Paris (Rodgers *et al.*, 1979). The First World War had drawn social workers into factory welfare with women workers and their children while men were at the front. In the aftermath of the war the public health campaigns against tuberculosis and childhood morbidity increased the roles of French social workers. The first schools of social work were established in 1905 in France, growing rapidly throughout the First World War and the 1920s, as they were in Germany (Schiller, 1983). These schools were originally outside the university system and were essentially women's colleges. A recent development across Europe has been the gradual inclusion of this training inside the public higher education system together with its expansion and increasing genericism from the 1960s, with post-qualifying and higher awards now being developed.

The final similarity is the 'crisis' since the 1974 oil crisis. Welfare states are accused by the right of creating a crisis through high expenditure, and of being in crisis because of rigid organisation and poor service delivery (often connected with apparently dominating professionals engaged in self-seeking expansion: see Flora, 1985). At the same time there has been a proliferation of often critical interest groups, speaking for users and would-be consumers; in short, a challenge from right to left to the *form* the state and state-sponsored welfare might take, a challenge heightened by a sense of recession and financial constraint. There was a critique of state intervention (and of the large 'private' welfare organisations) and of professional power from the libertarian left in the 1970s (see *Psychiatrica Democratica* in Italy: K. Jones, 1988; the German self-help and alternative groups: Brauns and Kramer, 1989; and radical social work in UK); and, more recently, by the libertarian right. Finally we should add that there is a crisis *for* the welfare state caused by changing labour markets and demographic changes in the family, both of which affect personal and domestic life and therefore have severe impact on the demand for social workers' services. A common response to these crises has been decentralisation and deinstitutionalisation, and the involvement of social workers in developing participation in new forms of welfare production and delivery. Because of a stronger tradition of pluralism in post-war European welfare states, British social workers have much to learn from their neighbours.

Principles: pluralism, subsidiarity, solidarity

The most obvious difference to a social worker visiting another European country is the extent of welfare pluralism: in the UK this has only recently (and not without difficulty) become a part of our community care and child-care systems, which remain dominated by large state organisations. In contrast, in much of western continental Europe, pluralism involves what are often referred to as private organisations: they are not public, but neither are they commercial, and are sometimes called independent or non-governmental organisations. Equivalent to our voluntary organisations, they often enjoy a more secure and institutionalised place in social welfare systems. Looking for exact equivalents is full of pitfalls, for social provision can be implemented by a variety of means: through public social services, through fiscal benefits (for example, tax concessions on housing, child care, etc.), and through occupational welfare (for example, in trade unions or firms: Mishra, 1981). The state (national and local), the market, the charitable, the independent, the informal (the family or community) are all means of delivering services, and states and governing parties promote and develop distinct welfare mixes.

In many northern European countries there appears to be a consensus that a plural system is one which promotes participation and self-help and acts as a buffer against a strong and potentially authoritarian state. It is the subsidiarity principle which enshrines this notion, evolving from the principles of individuality (self-reliance, personal dignity) and of solidarity (mutual bonds within society). Subsidiarity is a concept found in those member states whose welfare philosophies have drawn on Catholic social teaching to some extent, such as Ireland, but also Germany where we find a mix of Lutheran and Catholic influences, and France with its mixture of Catholic and republican traditions:

> Subsidiarity should be understood to mean that whatever smaller and more individual institutions (e.g. the family), groups (e.g. associations) or public bodies (e.g. communes, *Länder*, churches) can do on their own must not be taken from them by a higher level of competence or by the power of the state, but that responsibility should remain as near as possible to the people involved. At the same time there is a challenge to take on the tasks at the grass roots level if they can be carried out there instead of leaving them to superior agencies, (Lippa, 1983)

In Germany, France and the Netherlands public and 'private' agencies are strongly interwoven. 'Private' agencies provide much of the social, family and youth services, and are subject to state regulation as well as support. It is also a principle that the state should create the preconditions which allow smaller and more local units chances of development and the effective use and deployment of their resources; indeed, this is an *obligation* on the German state. Many of these private agencies will be Church organisations and some, like CARITAS (the Catholic social welfare agency) are very large international organisations. Others may be insurance funds which run social and health care services, including social work: for instance, the *Caisse d'allocations familiales* (CAF) in France. The fact of welfare pluralism then reveals the diversity of methods of service delivery and philosophy underlying social welfare, and the essentially local nature of much of the bargaining which takes place to establish welfare contracts.

The subsidiarity principle has already been shown to be closely tied to Catholic principles of social welfare. Catholic social teaching begins with the 1891 Encyclical *Rerum Novarum* on the condition of labour. The Church, of course, is a means by which social policies were linked across Europe. Various subsequent documents have been concerned with urbanisation, justice for the poor, solidarity with the poor, discrimination and marginalisation, migrants and human rights. According to Coote, Catholic social teaching asserts the value of human dignity, natural justice and the social obligations of ownership. Thus a 'legal or employment system which in fact results in discrimination against a particular ethnic group would offend against the responsibility of the state to work for the common good and against the fraternity or solidarity by which all citizens recognise one another as persons' (Coote, 1989, p. 155).

There is, then, a Catholic principle of the common good of the whole of society: society should not exclude on the grounds of poverty or property relations; co-ownership and participation of workers in public management are important in production for the use of all. Subsidiarity was delineated in 1931 by Pius XI:

> Just as individuals should not be prevented from performing their proper functions and responsibilities, by a transfer of these to the community, so higher bodies (including the state) should not take over functions which can be adequately carried out by lower and smaller bodies . . . Subsidiarity goes hand in hand with

the primary responsibility attributed to the state to reform the social order, and so acts as a limiting principle giving a proper place to other entities. It is part of the basis for rejecting collectivist systems, and also corporatist views of society such as those of contemporaneous Fascism in Italy. (Coote, 1989, p. 157)

Subsidiarity is not self-help in disguise because of its association with the concept of solidarity: it includes identification with and respect for others; a commitment to the common good and for each individual, between groups and of strong with weak, and the need for intermediate groups such as trade unions. Solidarity means more than the English notion of trade union fraternity, for it rests in the responsibility of each for all and in the notion of the socially responsible state. Within social policy it refers to social protection and social security, especially in France and Belgium where the insurance principle goes beyond individual contribution and protection to a mutualism and solidarity between state and individuals; to a general protection, if not redistribution (Schorr, 1965). It also refers to social cohesion and the provision of social work and social action as part of its creation or reinforcement, as a means of prevention or resolving social conflict. There is a similarity to Beveridge's notions of comprehensiveness and universalism, the pooling of social risks via national insurance and, while he did not use this term, French and Belgian texts and laws refer to his report (Spicker, 1991). Finally it refers to what is called social integration, altruism, or 'community' in Britain, and is the root of the contemporary French concern with *insertion* and exclusion (see Chapter 5) and the British concern with citizenship and social rights, which seem threatened by the apparent erosion of the welfare state. Spicker connects the ideas of solidarity and subsidiarity as follows:

Subsidiarity means that solidarity is hierarchically ordered; the main source of solidarity, or mutual responsibility is the family, second a community, and only at the end of the line the state. Solidarity is not diametrically opposed to subsidiarity in the way that institutional welfare is opposed to residual welfare. The picture that emerges, instead, is of progressively widening circles of responsibility, and of diminishing strength with social distance. (Spicker, 1990, p. 11)

It is this notion which provides a principle for the decentralisation, community care and self-help which have characterised welfare states during the 1980s. It is also a philosophy which marks a radical difference from British social policy, concerned as it is mainly with the relief of poverty and with individual need and deviance. By contrast continental philosophies, including conservative ones, view family support and child-care services as a social responsibility as well as a buttress to the family as the basic social institution (Spicker, 1991). It is this difference on the issue of social responsibility which meant that the British Conservative Party was not admitted to the centre right grouping at the European Parliament, the large and powerful European People's Party (EPP). This grouping of continental Christian Democrats has a fundamental commitment to European federalism and subsidiarity, to social solidarity and personal responsibility to family and community. Its social concern and Christian humanity made it hostile to Thatcherism (Hilton, 1990). The new Conservative administration under John Major in 1991 made forceful statements as to its commitment to social solidarity, the social market and regulation in the negotiations over its admission to the EPP.

While the northern European member states have, despite differences in histories and philosophies, developed roughly comparable institutionalised systems (if not levels) of provision, and have growing and increasingly professionalised personal social services, the 1980s also brought retrenchment and debate as to the directions which welfare should take. 'New' poverty and changes in the family have altered the quality and intensity of social work's tasks, and it is to the consumers of social work, and the classes from which they are drawn, that we now turn, bearing in mind that if solidarity is an aim of social policy, social work's mandate will derive from the perceived threat to social cohesion posed by economic and social marginalisation.

Contexts of social work

Poverty

One way in which the discourse on the 'crisis' in the welfare state has been handled is through the theme of the new poverty. While by the mid-1970s those with work records in the formal economy and their dependents were better protected and had higher living standards than in former times, groups who were not adequately insured became increasingly obvious, especially to social workers (who may be the source of discretionary help when universal services and insurance benefits are exhausted or unavailable). This is especially so in France and Belgium where social assistance (that is, discretionary benefits) is a local responsibility and where social workers may be involved in assessments or in supervising benefits. For example, Belgium's *Centres Public d'Aide Sociale* or France's *Centres Communal d'Action Sociale* (at local community level) have social workers who deal with first approaches for help (Leaper, 1988). Social assistance work may include social work with groups such as young people without work because of rising unemployment (and without insurance contributions), women with children but no (insured) husband, those who worked in the informal economy (often immigrants, often women, often single parents), elderly people without long work records (again often women), and the long-term unemployed in areas of industrial decline (mining, textiles, shipbuilding, etc.).

As the emergence of these poverty groups appeared to coincide with the slowdown of growth and the change in industrial patterns from old industries to new high-technology production, much of the research around this poverty has concentrated on assessing the changes in the labour market and their impact on women, youth and immigrants. In what the Germans refer to as the two-thirds/one-third society (Hamburger, 1989), it has become evident that there is a dual labour market: there are two classes of worker, one with good conditions, valued skills, affluence and mobility, and another on the periphery of the labour market suffering from an insecurity of employment terms and conditions, a precariousness. For immigrants it might mean 'voluntary' repatriation because they lack the means of staying in formal employment, or state-planned repatriation. 'Restructuring' has meant a widening of inequalities within the working class, and has fed the forces of racism and xenophobia by strengthening the processes which create the underclass. Women's participation in labour forces has grown everywhere, just as men's (and young men's) has fallen. Yet women are concentrated in part-time and temporary work and, while they may want stable and full-time work, it has been their 'flexibility' which has made them essential to the new production processes which require rapid change and adaptation to markets (Hagen and Jenson, 1988). Women are overwhelmingly concentrated in the growing service sector and public sector. Everywhere women earn less than men at hourly rates; single parents, female-headed households, divorced, separated and widowed women, and women from ethnic minorities are most at risk of unemployment and precariousness, underpinned by poor public child-care provision and maternity and parental leave. It is notable that those countries which are best in these areas – France and Sweden – are also those with the smallest earnings gap between men and women (Bakker, 1988).

How valid is the theory that what we see is *new* poverty and of what relevance is this for social workers? In all the EC countries poverty is a more significant issue than it was in the mid-1970s. In Britain the low level of social insurance benefits meant that the rediscovery of poverty via the large population forced to rely on social assistance came earlier. But in the other developed welfare states, those homeless or needing emergency relief, the growing numbers of single parents dependent on social assistance and the growth of debt have all been cited with anxiety. Such anxiety can reflect a moral concern – the loss of 'traditional' family values – or a concern with public order. In Germany, France and Belgium local government is responsible for the administration of social assistance, and local and locally-managed agencies have become acutely aware of increasing need (Leaper, 1988). The Catholic and Protestant churches have similarly expressed concern, as have trade unions (partly through fear of declining membership).

Poverty is notoriously difficult to measure in one country, let alone when making international comparisons, but in 1987 Room *et al.* (1989) coordinated a cross-country study of poverty in Europe concentrating on trends in numbers of people receiving social assistance. Dependency on social assistance has been rising rapidly in the majority of EC countries. The proportion (but not the number, which has not fallen) of elderly on social assistance is declining relative to those dependent through unemployment. In the long term the elderly proportion may rise again as those who suffered precarious employment become elderly. The proportion of large families dependent on social assistance is falling, especially in southern European countries, and the proportion of large families in Germany and the UK is small. The proportion of single people, employed people and single-parent families who are poor and dependent on social assistance is growing. The proportion of women on social assistance is falling but, in absolute numbers, female and female-headed household social assistance recipients have increased substantially in Belgium and Germany: the feminisation of poverty is clearly at work. Single-parent families are a high risk group, then, their risk having increased from the late 70's. Young people and ethnic minority groups are also at particular risk. Retrenchment in public expenditure has hit these groups hard: for instance, in Germany social assistance rates fell significantly and eligibility criteria were toughened from the mid-1970s. Southern and peripheral states of the EC have doubly suffered in this process, both because of already existing rural poverty, but now also because of declining opportunities to migrate and new unemployment caused by returning migrants from Germany and other richer countries. Room concludes from his survey that the term 'new' poverty is to some extent a mystification. While the phrase 'new poverty' is useful in mobilising governments, poverty is not new and it is not a new thing to have an underclass. What is new is the widening of the range of the population subject to economic insecurity.

Migration, racism and xenophobia

Something like 30 million people entered western European countries as workers or their dependents in the post-war period, and many migrated within Europe (usually from the south of Italy and from Portugal, Spain and Ireland to the prosperous north). All West European countries restricted the entry of workers from 1973–4, the British government having begun earlier in 1962. There are strikingly similar patterns of arrival and settlement. Most early migrant workers arrived with the aim of saving enough to return home to a better life. Poverty traps, inflation and entry restrictions meant that such hopes declined, and families gradually joined their men. Second (and now third) generations have been born in Europe; the younger people retain more tenuous links with their parents' or grandparents' countries of origin, though there are recent strong movements for cultural self-determination. Despite citizenship, for example in the Netherlands, Britain and France, or at least (for some) the right to stay (in Germany), ethnic minority groups protest that they are made to feel outsiders by their segregation in poor housing and jobs, and the racism that they experience in their daily lives (Castles, 1984).

In France the young French-born of North African descent – known as Beurs – have a particularly sharp sense of exclusion, heightened by blocked aspirations (Hargreaves, 1989). France has now around a million young citizens of North African origin who have become the focus of intense public debate during the 1980s. The right wing (led by le Pen) argues that the high birth rate (it is actually declining) of North African families will swamp the French nation and culture; they talk of the 'threat' of Islam. So, as in the UK or Germany, a foreign population has shifted from being predominantly male to a more balanced sex ratio, and has become younger. The ways in which schools should respond to issues of language, religious teaching and culture (for example, girls covering their heads) has become a matter of debate, but the socialist government which came to power in 1981 has promoted the idea of *insertion*: that is, integration into society with a right to difference rather than colonial assimilation and loss of cultural identity. Exclusion has been as a political threat, and activists (such as Harlem Desir of SOS Racisme) have become powerful voices.

However, despite such hopes and huge renovation and social action schemes in the massive housing estates which ring French cities and in which 'immigrants' tend to be concentrated, there has been disorder in Lyons and Paris. Much urban policy has been undermined by the right (for instance, in Marseilles), by the Centre-Right government of 1986–8, and by the differences within the left. It has been the Socialist Party and Mitterrand who have given voice to the Beur generation, to SOS Racisme and to Banlieues 1989 (the former concentrating on educational policy and the latter on the renovation of estates). These large French estates are often in jobless zones, have 'social cases' housed alongside a high proportion of 'immigrant' families, and are generally accepted as high in crime and anxiety, and low on opportunities (French social action will be discussed more fully in Chapter 5).

A study of young Turks in Germany found that only a minority of them and their parents were happy to live in Germany and, while material gain was given as the advantage of migration, the

> disadvantages listed were more social and psychological, such as homesickness, being away from home, weakening of family ties. They expressed these disadvantages in serious tones, giving the impression that they believed the material gains could not compensate for the psychosocial harm. 90% felt that the Turkish workers in West Germany suffer greatly . . . The proportion of those feeling disliked by the Germans was very high (93%) whether or not this was actually the case, they were disturbed by feeling so. It was particularly important that they felt they were disliked more than other immigrant workers. (Kosar, 1988, p. 271)

Refugees were a rapidly growing group at the start of the 1990s, and are likely to become larger and of more concern to social workers. Third World refugees are being joined by refugees from Eastern Europe and the Soviet Union in a massive movement of people, who are finding the boundaries of the EC increasingly tightened. In the UK refugee groups such as Tamils, Eritreans, Somalis and Kurds have recently grown. Social services departments are accused of not fulfilling their responsibilities, which tend to be pushed back to voluntary agencies and the Church, with the refugee community associations often bearing the brunt of the welfare and legal rights and resettlement work on shoe-string budgets. There has been a 400 per cent increase in applications for asylum from 1988 to 1990 and it is the hardest-pressed London boroughs – Hackney, Haringey, and Camden – that tend to receive refugees. The British Refugee Council has demanded central government funding to local authorities for specific housing allocations to refugee-supporting boroughs, and the extension of Section 11 funding to allow local authorities to employ specialist staff and to assist voluntary organisations. Such prospects seem a long way off, however (Redding, 1990), and indeed because of the fear of further black/Third World immigration the government is intent on tightening entry controls and procedures (for instance, by fining airlines carrying passengers without right of entry, and by stiffer assessments of whether people face legitimate fear of persecution).

The former West Germany has, because its constitution allowed entry to refugees and because of its strong economy, the highest proportion of refugees in the EC. In Dusseldorf, for instance, there is a 12 per cent foreign population, and in 1989 there were 8000 new arrivals from East Germany and 'ethnic' Germans from Poland. The figures were exceeded in 1990. These 'new' Germans have, unlike Third World refugees, the right to German citizenship, yet even these groups experience increasing resentment from local populations and a long wait for housing and jobs. Third World asylum seekers have a far more marginal position; they live on social assistance, are not allowed to work and are forced into the informal, underground economy. In 1989 141 000 and in 1990 200 000 asylum-seekers (of whom two-thirds are non-European) were allowed into Germany, and from these groups an underclass even below the now settled

Turkish groups (who at least have a position, even if precarious, in the formal economy) is being created. The German government has pressed for a common EC policy through burden-sharing and common visa policies. Meanwhile the social welfare services which foreign workers and their families receive tends to come from *Arbeiterwohlfahrt* (a non-denominational social democratic welfare organisation) which has a network of welfare provision run by social pedagogues (that is, social workers with an educative/creative role), such as after-school schemes: it has 32 out-of-school centres in Dusseldorf (Jarvis, 1990c).

Strong-arm tactics complete the picture of 'fortress Europe' where equal opportunities legislation for EC citizens is combined with strong controls on immigration at strengthened EC borders: the Austrian army has begun patrolling the Austro-Hungarian border with jeeps and helicopters, seeking to thwart illegal immigrants from the poorest countries of Eastern Europe (Bulgaria, Romania and Poland) and abandoning its open-door policy which allowed more than 2.5 million people to obtain asylum since 1945 (*The Independent*, 3 January 1991). At the same time the Eastern European countries are fearful of immigration from the former Soviet Union, and are considering their own border controls. It is this great human movement which will present social work with a tremendous challenge in the 1990s and, because of its international nature, will perhaps draw together social workers from different countries.

Family diversity

While there has always been diversity in family structures, it seems the 'classic' nuclear family is everywhere declining as a proportion of households (Rapoport, 1989). For many families headed by women, or with an unemployed man, poverty will be a consequence of the continued disadvantage of women in terms of pay and conditions as well as of inadequate support services and of insurance systems based on the wage-earning husband. States do vary, however, in their levels of provision and support for women in their caring roles. Day care for children, the disabled and elderly people; after-school and holiday care for children; respite care and home-care schemes (benefits in kind) and child allowances; invalid care allowances; holiday vouchers; tax exemptions, and associated rights like leave for family reasons, protection of pension rights if out of the labour force to care for a relative; all these may, to varying degrees, mitigate or exacerbate the burdens of women and enrich or diminish the lives of children, the elderly and disabled people.

Family policies contain ideological attitudes and different attitudes to the 'privacy' of the family and to children as future national capital. Some countries at particular times have extended benefits to families when the birth rate or the quality of the population seemed threatened (for instance, in the infant welfare movement in the early twentieth century, or after the First World War). Natalist attitudes have often occurred alongside anxiety about the working-class family and its supposed fragility; from this conjuncture has grown social work and an emphasis on the responsibility of parents as a condition for their privacy and their parental rights (Meyer, 1983). Extremes of natalism occured under Nazism or Vichy France, when family policies were designed to produce more citizens from particular social groups (Hartman, 1984).

The British tradition is one that asserts the privacy and responsibility of the family, and seeks to restrict state 'interference.' The distaste for natalist and strong family support policies has legitimated a neglect and relative disadvantage of the family in Britain. For instance, while single mothers tend in Europe (and the USA) to be poorer than married couples with children, in the UK

23% of single mothers with one child and 32% of those with two or more children had an . . . income . . . of less than 50% of the median in the country . . . In comparison the corresponding figures for married couples were 2% and 13%. (In the US the differences are even larger). Contrast this with the situation in Holland (and Sweden) where single mothers still are more likely to be poor than are couples with children, but where the differences are substantially smaller. In Holland, for example, 10 per cent of single mothers and 9 per cent of couples with one child had adjusted family incomes of less than half the median in Holland. (Sorensen, 1989)

In Germany, 9 per cent of single mothers have an adjusted family income of less than half the median.

The way the state regulates maintenance payments from husbands, women's earnings rates and public child care produces different outcomes for single mothers in different member states. In 1989, in calling for the establishment of a network to be known as the European Family Policy Observatory, the Commission of the EC noted demographic and socio-economic changes:

> The last decades have been marked by profound demographic and socio-economic changes, from which no Community country is immune, even if the changes take place with certain time delays and at different rhythms.
>
> In short, the demographic trend is characterised by a lower fertility rate, an increase in life expectancy resulting in an ageing population, which will decline in the medium term. This change in age structure of the population will be accompanied by a change in family structure, a result of the decline in marriage and of the increase in numbers of divorces. The restructuring of the labour market, changes in working conditions and increase in female labour participation are the principal factors in this new economic landscape. (Commission of EC, 1989a, p. 15).

Family structures are becoming more diverse, with reconstituted families, single-parent families and unions 'by agreement' increasing. Large families are declining, although they remain more prevalent in southern Europe. One-person households are increasing throughout the EC (30 per cent of all in Denmark and the former West Germany, as opposed to about 12 per cent in Spain, Portugal and Greece); most are women. Women face difficulties in reconciling work and family life, while work and training opportunities offer women the possibilities of independence. Economic restructuring may, after 1992, make some families more vulnerable while bringing new employment opportunities for others. The idea of the Observatory is to facilitate the inclusion of the family dimension in EC policies: for instance, in the freedom of movement of persons and equality between men and women; to assess the impact of other community policies on the family; to make measures on equal opportunities more effective; and to make measures in favour of families more tailored to the characteristics and difficulties of some families.

The Commission argues that child-care facilities are a key component of family policies, echoing the report of the Childcare Network (Moss, 1988). Provision does not match demand anywhere and the quality is uneven; and while provision for children of 0–3 is a priority, from 3 to 10 is also a necessity. The argument of the Commission is that children are becoming more rare and the family must be protected for the cohesion and future of society. EC states vary in attitudes to the family: eight have family rights enshrined in national constitutions, and four (France, Luxemburg, Portugal and Germany) have a Minister for the Family, as do the three Belgian communities and some of the German *Länder*. Some states have no official family policy at all, while others have an explicit family policy as a keystone of society. The Preamble to the Single European Act contains a declaration on the protection of the family, but it is evident that views on the means of doing so vary.

Conclusion

While social trends are remarkably similar in patterns of migration and settlement and in family and household changes across Europe, and while there are common anxieties about social problems (youth and crime, single parenthood, poverty and family stress), there are great variations in policies and their direct and indirect impact on individuals, groups and families. This chapter has shown some of the difficulties in making comparisons between social welfare systems: if we compare only on empirical grounds and do not look at the legitimating principles which lie behind them, we may become confused in assessing their effectiveness, or in grasping the varied means of delivering services.

If social solidarity is an important goal, and if it is understood in dynamic terms as the reciprocal relations between groups, institutions and the state, then the social work task can be seen to be important in promoting social cohesion. In Britain social work tends to see its task as the meeting of individual need, and less (though latently) as the protection or development of society as a whole. Indeed, such a goal is one many social workers would resist, feeling that it is not their job to fit people into society. And perhaps that can be the danger of policies which stress the development of the state and nation. Yet the principles of solidarity and subsidiarity give social work a broader, preventive and community development mandate: not to separate individuals from society, but to promote healthy relations between and within groups, and to see that as a process of encouraging participation of the marginalised from below, aided by resources from above. Interesting issues of accountability are raised, as we shall see later in the book in discussions about social action and participation, but first we examine the organisation and branches of social work in other European states.

3

Social Workers, Organisations and the State

Introduction

Contemporary social work in the member states of the EC has developed in the context of a range of cultural and philosophical traditions and socio-economic conditions (see Chapter 2). This chapter considers some aspects of the organisational bases from which social work is practised, and related issues concerning the training and professional status of social workers; it also attempts to identify some of the similarities and contrasts. An indication will be given of the relative importance of the different *sectors* involved in provision of social services and in which social workers are employed. Thus we will consider the roles of the state, the Church, the voluntary sector (non-profit making, non-governmental organisations), the private (commercial) sector, and the informal sector (including self-help groups) in selected countries (Greece, Ireland, Germany, Denmark, Spain and the Netherlands) and some general themes will be identified.

First, however, it may be useful to consider the definition of social services since the term cannot be automatically equated with Personal Social Service Departments as established in England and Wales since 1970. Munday, in a report of a meeting of social services representatives from member states held in 1989, reported on an agreed definition of the basic characteristics, paraphrased as follows:

1. work undertaken by social workers, but also other occupational groups, and possibly volunteers;
2. services provided for client groups including elderly people, people with physical and/or mental disabilities or mental health problems, children and families, and sometimes young and adult offenders;
3. services provided through fieldwork and in domiciliary, day care or residential settings, with some trend towards 'community care';
4. a selective rather than universal service aimed at individuals, clients or users with particular needs;
5. work aimed at achieving change (whether in human relationships and/or social environment); providing social support and/or control; and protecting civil rights.

By this definition (Munday, 1990) all EC countries can be judged to have some form of state social service provision – that is, service provided by local authorities (or by voluntary agencies with state mandate and funding) – and a statutory basis for specified activities and provisions. Thus in all EC countries social work receives a mandate from the state and is recognised as carrying out certain activities on behalf of society. However, in so far as national views of the nature of society and the role and form of 'welfare states' vary, so do the powers and expectations placed on social work. As we have indicated, pluralist systems in some countries, such as the Netherlands and Germany, have a relatively long tradition, partly related (in Germany at least) to the principle of *subsidiarity*, which is the provision of help at the lowest level or by the least formal means, such as through family and informal care first, or by voluntary or private agencies, in preference to statutory services. This also relates to the basis for funding.

Rather than engage in a series of generalisations about the role of the state and the place of other sectors at the EC level, it may be helpful to move on to a series of thumbnail sketches of some of the major characteristics of social work organisation and social services provision in the six selected countries.

Greece

The development of social work and social services in Greece has taken place mainly since the Second World War. The country has experienced rural depopulation (35 per cent of the population lived in rural areas according to the 1981 Census), and possesses limited natural resources and a small industrial/manufacturing base. The post-war period has seen major political changes, from Communist uprisings and civil war, through constitutional monarchy, to a military regime and the re-establishment of a civilian government in 1974, and then a significant political shift to the right with the election of the New Democracy Party in 1990.

The development of social services has been closely related to the post-war establishment of a national health service, and both services are the responsibility of the Ministry of Health and Welfare. The early 1980s were a period of Socialist government with attempts at economic and social planning. Thus, a five year plan from 1983 to 1987 included developments in both areas which resulted in an increase in provisions, such as day care facilities for children under school age; residential care establishments; and health centres (all potential bases for social work services). The majority (90 per cent) of Greece's 3700 social workers (who are registered by the Ministry of Health and Welfare) operate in public social welfare agencies, funded by national government but administered regionally (J. King, 1990a). The public sector gained significant ground in the 1980s but there continue to exist a number of Church-run establishments, such as orphanages and other residential facilities, alongside those run by other organisations in the voluntary sector, including the Red Cross. Following a period of government preference for state provision, constraints on public expenditure and changed political control have led to the potential contributions of the private (commercial) sector receiving more attention. However, as yet it is not a significant employer of social workers or provider of services.

Social workers mainly operate in relation to particular client groups (see Chapter 4) and generally offer assessment and direct services to individuals and families. They are involved in the administration of public assistance and in relation to public housing, and may also work with self-help organisations (for example, in relation to drugs). Both case work and community development models have influenced their practice, and the latter is particularly relevant to work in rural areas. During the 1980s two pieces of legislation (N1262/82 and N1622/86) and some reallocation of funding all aimed to increase citizen participation at community and regional level. The legislation provided for the establishment of Development Associations eligible for funding from the state and the EC. However, Stathopoulos has commented on the relatively slow growth of these Associations, and their apparently limited success in encouraging participation. He further suggests that programmes tend to be focused around specific services, so community (social) workers have no mandate to promote social rights (advocacy is seen as being the domain of politicians and labour organisations: Stathopoulos, 1991). Indeed, there may even be concern about whether social workers promote or protect human rights: for example, in relation to the treatment of Turkish and other minority groups when they need public and social services (Markopoulou, 1990).

While social workers have limited legal responsibilities and relatively low status and career prospects (related to training: see below), their views are sought and taken into account by other regulatory bodies, such as the courts. Social workers in Greece may find themselves working in comparative isolation from each other, and opportunities for supervision and professional development are fairly limited. About 1525 of them belong to the Greek Association of Social Workers (established in 1955) which attempts to represent the interests of social workers and their clients to the government and to organise conferences, meetings and other forms of professional support. It also seeks to improve social workers' pay and conditions of service (although it is not a union), and enforces (with the Ministry of Health and Welfare) a Code of Ethics dating from 1960.

Training

Of the current social work force 95 per cent is female, and 70 per cent are under 40 years of age. The majority (90 per cent) obtained their training in Greece, on a $3^{1}/_{2}$ year (seven semester) training course at one of Greece's three Departments of Social Work (Athens, Crete and Patras). These are based in the Technological Education Institutes (TEIs) which are at tertiary education level but generally considered of a lower status than the university sector. Graduates of the TEIs in public employment are on lower rates of pay and have fewer opportunities for advancement than university-trained counterparts from other disciplines, and social workers cannot therefore normally become welfare managers, for instance.

Recruitment to social work training is on the basis of grades obtained in national examinations at 18 years, and approximately half the entrants have not identified social work as a first choice of course. Students are allocated to courses, rather than selected on the basis of suitability for social work. However, there is a relatively low wastage rate, and the courses produce about 80 social workers per annum. Courses follow a national curriculum established in 1983 and include a practice element, with the final semester in employment. There is a small number of unemployed social workers at present, but conversely the Greek Association considers that the overall number of workers is insufficient and should be increased to 5000. It is also concerned to promote opportunities for post-qualifying training and to see the status of training (for example, transfer into the university sector) and of the profession improved.

Republic of Ireland

Despite some similarities to the UK in its social work origins (for example, state provisions originally determined by the 1834 Poor Law), Irish social work has developed in the twentieth century in a very different national, political and economic context. As a largely rural country, major elements in the post-war situation have been strenuous efforts to encourage the development of modern industries, and also of the education and training sector. However, continuing fluctuations in the economy and quite widespread unemployment and poverty (about one-third of the population is currently dependent on social welfare payments) have led to a continuing pattern of emigration of both unskilled workers and trained professionals (including to EC institutions). The Catholic church has continued to play an important role in the social and political life of the country, including the welfare sector, and there is also a long tradition of voluntary activity, self-help, cooperative ventures, local fund-raising, and informal care.

There are currently less than 1000 social workers in Ireland, of whom about three-fifths are employed in the state sector (309 in eight Regional Health Boards, 163 in the Department of Justice and 70 in local authorities: see Reive, 1987). Social workers employed by the Health Boards usually work in teams (which may include a community worker) and may be based in health centres, hospitals or separate welfare offices. They are primarily concerned with statutory child-care work, although they may also undertake work in the mental health field. They are responsible for determining needs and resources, and monitoring their own plans and budgets, but there are relatively few opportunities for career progression beyond senior social worker level since teams are normally part of community care sections within the Health Structure, managed by people with medical qualifications. The community care concept in Ireland includes public health provisions (prevention of infectious diseases and health education); primary health care services (GPs, home nursing; dental, ophthalmic and aural services); and social welfare (social work, financial assistance to individuals and grants to voluntary welfare agencies: see J. King, 1990b). Financial assistance is administered by Community Welfare Officers who are not normally social workers, and who work in a separate administrative unit, although social workers have contact with them as advocates. In 1990 a Government Commission on Regional Health Boards made various recommendations for financial and structural changes, with (at the time of writing) unresolved implications for social workers. There have also been recent cuts in government spending, and legislative changes (for example, in child care) which impinge on the role and responsibilities of statutory social workers.

The voluntary sector comprises 156 organisations, at national and local level, and many of these, together with the Church, provide the bulk of social work, residential and community care (through domiciliary and day care) services for people who are elderly and/or have disabilities. In addition, some social workers are directly employed by voluntary hospitals, and a small number work in voluntary child care agencies or (an even smaller number) in occupational social work.

Training

About 40 per cent of all social workers belong to the Irish Association of Social Workers or IASW (established in 1971), and many belong to one of two unions (which are voting on amalgamation). Plans are proceeding for the registration of social workers, possibly through the IASW. Most social workers have been trained on one of three social work courses (at University College, Cork, University College, Dublin or Trinity College, Dublin) which are comparable to social work training courses in the UK (and until 1988 were approved by the Central Council of Education & Training in Social Work, (CCETSW)). A new national body is currently being established to approve courses, and there is some emphasis on the promotion of three-year (degree) courses to meet EC Directive requirements (see discussion below). It is also hoped to develop post-qualifying training opportunities.

Germany

Following the early development of a welfare system at the turn of the century (including the establishment in 1916 of the DVS, the German Association for Female Welfare Officers), German social work experienced a period of decline and subversion in the 1930s and 1940s. The current welfare system and redevelopment of social work dates from 1949 when the Basic Law (*Grundgesetz*) prescribed a social role for the state, and the principle of subsidiarity (see Chapter 2) was given constitutional form. National factors which currently impinge on the role of social workers and on the development of social services are an ageing population, some economic and social dislocation associated with the reunification of Germany, increasing unemployment rates (particularly of young people and migrants) and increased demands on social welfare. Although only one in twenty of the population is dependent on state benefits, a relatively high proportion live below the poverty line according to the EC definition of having less than half the national average income. This situation of relative poverty occurs in a country with generally high costs and standards of living. With reference to social welfare, the Federal Public Assistance Act of 1962 intended that certain categories of people not adequately covered by social insurance schemes would be legally entitled to financial assistance (*Sozialhilfe*) and associated social work help from the state, via municipalities. However, this legislation assumed a situation of economic growth and near full employment, and 35–50 per cent of those now claiming social assistance are unemployed (Weghaus, 1990). There is also concern about the relatively low take-up of entitlement (F. Hooper, 1987) related to lack of information, the intrusive nature of enquiries about eligibility, and inadequate social work help to applicants, attributed in part at least to attempts by municipalities to limit their own public spending levels.

As just indicated, a proportion of German social workers is employed by the state at local level. The exact numbers of social workers in Germany and relative proportions are not available. There are three levels of legislation and administration within Germany: federal (which establishes the legal framework for most welfare and public provisions); regional (*Länder*, which have a high degree of autonomy in policy making, within the state framework); and local urban or county authorities (*Kreis*, which have relatively large powers for administering resources, including disbursement of state funds to voluntary bodies and direct provision of services). The principle of subsidiarity already referred to means, for instance, that the local authority can only set up a residental home for elderly people if no organisation in the voluntary or private sector is willing to do so. However, certain legal duties are ascribed to the local authorities in relation to youth and child welfare, guardianship and probation, although even these can be delegated to voluntary agencies in some circumstances (see next chapter).

Local authority social services have three main roles:

1. to identify and assess people for material help, including special circumstances;
2. to provide child protection and youth welfare services (though some provisions may be encouraged through the voluntary sector);
3. to carry out preventive health measures (Jarvis, 1990b).

The other major streams of social work and service provision within the state system are those related to the courts and penal system (probation), and to public health and hospital services. Many of the services provided to elderly people, for instance, are actually provided on health grounds, and on the basis of medical insurance, rather than being assessed as social needs (Hantrais, Mangen and O'Brien, 1990). Overall, state social work is seen as taking place within a bureaucratic framework, with professional practice being limited by administrative requirements and increased demands in relation to financial assistance.

Returning to the principle of support to voluntary organisations and cooperation between the state and the voluntary sector, it is not surprising that the other major employers of social workers and providers of services is the voluntary sector, including churches. An estimated 800 000 social workers and 1.5 million volunteers (including conscientious objectors who may undertake fifteen months' social service instead of one year's military service) are employed by the 'Big Six' major welfare cartels: *Deutscher Caritasverband* and

Diakonischeswerk des Evangelischen Kirche in Deutschland (Catholic and Protestant German Welfare Organisations); *Zentrale Wolfahrtstelle der Juden in Deutschland* (Jewish Welfare); *Arbeiterwohlfahrt* (Workers' Welfare); *Deutscher Paritätischer Wohlfahrtsverband* (an umbrella group for nondenominational non-political organisations); and *Deutsches Rotes Kreuz* (the German Red Cross: see Flamm, 1980). The 1980s also saw a growth in the number of small voluntary organisations (partly arising out of the self-help movement), although recent changes in funding arrangements have given a renewed stimulus to the Big Six. There has also been some relative growth in the private sector, and this plays a fairly important part in provision of residential care.

There are currently two social work associations in Germany: *Deutscher Berufsverband der Sozialarbeiter und Sozialpädagogen* or DBS (the German Professional Association of Social Workers and Social Educators), and the *Berufsverband der Sozialarbeiter, Sozialpädagogen und Heilpädagogen* or BSH (Professional Association of Social Workers, Social Educators and Therapeutic Educators). However, a relatively small proportion of social workers belong to these organisations (possibly less than 10 per cent) and a number belong to other trade unions. Overall, the levels of pay of social workers are not as good as other professional groups (such as teachers), and there are both limits on German social workers' career possibilities (for example, they are not normally qualified to become managers in local authority social services, or social work teachers), and there is a relatively large number of unemployed social workers (nearly 20 000 in 1986, although unification opened up new possibilities for social work employment and numbers have reduced).

Training

The last point relates directly to the training system for social work which consists mainly of three-year courses in the *Fachhochschulen* (higher education institutions with technical and vocational bias), and to a lack of selection and control over numbers: anyone with sufficient academic grades is entitled to take a course. Thus 7000 or 8000 social workers graduate from the *Fachhochschulen* annually, either from *Sozialarbeit* or *Sozialpädagogik* courses, approved by the *Länder*. The difference between *Sozialarbeit* (training social workers for therapeutic, curative and remedial interventions, such as with children and families) and *Sozialpädagoge* (training social workers in an educative, preventative and developmental mode: for example, for work with young people and in communities; see Chapter 4) is longstanding but does not necessarily determine the posts which social workers subsequently occupy, and there is current emphasis on integrating the training, the first three semesters (half the course) now being taught jointly. There is considerable diversity between courses in different *Länder* and some criticism of them as lacking structural perspectives and practical experience. Some courses do not have placements as such but students undertake project work (which can result in local innovative developments and cooperation between academic institutions and the community), and are only qualified on completion of a fourth year's probationary period. Other *Länder* favour four-year courses incorporating a practical period. There has also been the development (since 1969) of four-year training programmes in a few universities. Apart from issues related to the training, employment and status of social workers, there are also increasing concerns about the representation and participation of consumers in social work and social services provisions, and the need for greater acknowledgement of cultural diversity within the German population.

Denmark

One of the smallest countries in the EC (in both area and population), Denmark, also has one of the longest established democratic constitutions (dating from 1849), and a well-developed state welfare sector (initiated in the late nineteenth century). Demographically, its population represents a near average in EC terms (21.1 per cent or its children are under 15 years and 13 per cent of its people are aged over 65) but in other respects it differs significantly. With the highest proportion of its population (including women) in employment, and the highest Gross Domestic Product (GDP) (relative to population) in the EC, it constitutes the most prosperous example of an advanced economy with the highest level of public spending. Nevertheless, as in other national examples, there has been recent concern about levels of welfare expenditure and also about the increasing proportion of people (young and/or unemployed) dependent on state benefits. The traditionally high level of public services provision has included the development of social services, and about two-thirds of the country's 6000 or more social workers are now employed in the state sector. Social services were the responsibility of the Ministry of Health and Social Welfare until 1970, then were organised regionally for a period (when bureaucratisation threatened professional identity and practice), and since 1979 they have been the responsibility of relatively small local authorities (275 municipalities). Central government still meets 50 per cent of local expenditure and pays all pensions, but the Ministry of Health and Social Welfare now has a relatively limited role, including no power to enforce minimum standards (Philpot, 1989). At local level, social workers work in departments which span health and welfare (including financial payments), and there has recently been some restructuring aimed at increasing specialisation. There is a general expectation that social services should operate on a community basis and in a preventive way, and there is a relatively longstanding acceptance of the principles of consumer representation; normalisation; and integration (dating from the 1950s and 1960s in the fields of 'special' education and residential care of the elderly). There is also a clearly stated policy on 'community care': that is, legislation and services aimed at enabling people to remain in their own homes for as long as possible and at improving the quality of life of 'clients' and their carers. For instance, a relatively high proportion of elderly people receive domiciliary services (17 per cent home help and 12 per cent home nursing), and over half the authorities provide 24-hour services. Efforts are also being made to reduce the number of elderly people in residential care through increased adaptation of local authority housing and home care services (see

A. Jamieson in Hantrais, Mangen and O'Brien, 1990). Child-care and child protection services are also provided through local authority departments, and social workers are employed in Probation Departments.

With state care accepted as the norm and social care seen as a right comparable with medical care, it is hardly surprising that social service provision through the Church, the voluntary sector, private and self-help sectors is relatively less in evidence. However, the state does provide financial assistance to voluntary organisations geared to the needs of particular user groups, providing field social work, residential and day care services (for instance, for people with cerebral palsy) and there is also a small amount of contracting of residential care from the private sector. In relation to residential care, an interesting aspect of provision is the relatively widespread use of multi-purpose facilities catering for people of different ages and with different types of handicap, although there are also examples of specialised provision, such as facilities catering for children who have been subject to neglect or abuse.

Training

The majority of Danish social workers belong to the professional association, *Dansk Socialradgiverforening* or DS (Association of Danish Social Workers) established in 1949, which also operates as a union, and all but 300 qualified social workers are registered by it. Most social workers are mature women (the average age of entry to training being relatively high, 28 years) and training takes place in five schools of social work, located in the universities (Copenhagen, Aarhus and Esbjerg), or affiliated (Ahlborg), or at the Institute of Social Studies (Philpot, 1990). Courses have been 3–3^1/$_2$ years long since the late 1950s, with fairly uniform curricula. The first school of social work was established in 1937, to train staff to operate in the (then new) material aid centres, and the courses now aim to produce generically trained social workers. Entry to courses is based on relatively high academic requirements and a minimum of nine months' previous paid work; the Ministry of Education sets annual intake figures (reduced from nearly 400 per annum in the early 1980s to less than 300 by 1985, but showing some increase to 350 by 1990). Nevertheless, there is a relatively high rate of unemployment among social workers (4.7 per cent). There is also concern, voiced by DS, that, given the generally high standard of living, a good standard of services and an orientation towards community care, the needs of particular minorities (such as people experiencing addictions or homelessness) should not be neglected, and social workers should maintain their traditional role as protectors and promoters of the rights and interests of minorities.

Spain

Third only to Germany and France in size and with a population of nearly 40 million, Spain has the highest proportion of land area still under agricultural use or wooded, and the third lowest population density in the EC after Greece and Ireland. It remains a predominantly Catholic country at the individual level, although the place of the Church has to some extent changed alongside major political changes in the twentieth century. With only just over half of the average GDP and the highest unemployment rate in the EC, Spain has been making efforts to develop its economy and its welfare system, particularly during the 1980s. However, one outcome of this (familiar elsewhere) has been a widening gap between those in work (the 'haves') and the unemployed (the 'have nots'). Following Franco's death in 1975, and the ending of a long period of military rule, democracy was re-established and a new constitution proclaimed in 1978. Since that time, social services developments have been the responsibility of seventeen *autonomias* (autonomous regions), and priority has been given to the creation of primary care services (Rossell and Rimbau, 1989). The *Ministerio de Asuntos Sociales* (Ministry of Social Affairs) was established in 1978 and this now oversees plans, monitors services and ensures compliance.

The aim has been to develop free, universal social services based on need and delivered by qualified social workers, and there has been a significant growth both in the range of services and the number of social workers employed by the state at local level (475 in Catalonia in 1982, but 1722 by 1987). In developing social services, account was taken of other models (particularly those of Scotland and Italy) and the services provided are closely integrated into the primary care network, incorporating health, education and culture. Following a period in the 1970s when social workers were active in raising civic consciousness and organising neighbourhood associations and other forms of community development, current social work practice is (still) based on the principles of decentralisation, participation, normalisation and integration. Significant progress has been achieved over the past decade and much social legislation has been enacted (concerning, for instance, minors, adoption and people with disabilities), but recent progress has been hampered by the reduction in public sector budgets. Additionally, state services have been criticised as bureaucratic, inefficient and discouraging participation.

In the light of all this, a relative reaction against provision of welfare services by the Church, voluntary and private sectors (which were long established and predominant in the Franco era) is now being re-evaluated. The role and relationship of major organisations, such as CARITAS and the Red Cross, to state services is now being seriously discussed, and there has been some renewed growth of self-help activities (for example, cooperatives) among particular groups such as unemployed people (sometimes with the support of a voluntary organisation such as CARITAS). Indeed, a form of welfare pluralism is being developed almost before the public social services had fully developed (Rossell and Rimbau in Munday, 1989). Throughout, the family has been seen as an important resource (in relation to care of children under school age, and people who are ageing and/or with a disability). However, the extended family has largely given way to nuclear family units and there has been some growth in domiciliary and day care relative to total care by the family or in institutions.

Training

About 70 per cent of Spain's social workers belong to the national professional Association, *Consejo General de Colegios Oficiales de Diplomados en Trabajor Social y Asistentes Sociales* (founded in 1967). The Association keeps a register of its members who must hold a university diploma, and the profession is regulated by the state. Almost 90 per cent of social workers are female and, given the rapid growth in numbers in the past decade, the age profile is relatively young. Training dates from 1932 when a School of Social Studies for Women was established, but there has been a re-emergence of the profession and of training opportunities in the postwar period. In 1964 the 32 schools of social work were awarded the same status as teaching and nursing training and, in 1970, 29 of the schools were affiliated to the Church (Stone, 1990). Social work education is now established as a three-year diploma at university level. However, it is not possible for students to obtain degrees in social work and thus, as in some other countries, career prospects may be limited. A national study programme has been devised by the Ministry of Education; students in different schools (some still supported by the Church) follow a common curriculum, often taught by part-time staff who are also employed in local social services.

Despite concerns about the effects of economic constraint, the territorial inequalities caused by the high degree of autonomy given to the regions and uncertainty about the future relationship between state and non-governmental agencies, there have been significant advances in the provision of social services since the late 1970s, and social work itself seems infused with a sense of youthful enthusiasm.

The Netherlands

This small country has the highest population density in the EC, near-average dependency rates (children under fifteen and adults over 65) and an above average standard of living. It is known for its progressive attitudes and legislation on drugs, prostitution, abortion and euthanasia, but also has a relatively high level of commitment to the Church (fairly evenly divided between Catholic and Protestant traditions) and the family. The roots of social service provision derive from Church welfare organisations, but in the post-war period the Dutch have constructed a sophisticated welfare state involving direct provision of social services by the voluntary and private sector, with financial support and regulation of standards from central and local government, and mostly funded by insurance (Lunn, 1990). In 1989, 10 per cent of the Gross National Product (GNP) was spent on health and welfare, and efforts have been made to reduce this. There is general support for an insurance system which meets both health and welfare needs, but disagreement (between Socialist and Liberal parties) as to whether this should be a national or private system (Cohen, 1990a). While social services are the responsibility of the Ministry of Welfare, Health and Cultural Affairs (which employs some social workers), the administration of them is divided between eleven provinces, four large cities, and local town councils.

Additionally, social workers are employed by the Department of Justice (the Child Protection Board) to undertake statutory child-care work, and in probation work. The Netherlands is comparable with the UK and Ireland in its relatively limited provision of child care for children under school age, but is unique in the EC in having a high level of residential care for people over 65 (12 per cent), originally established as a response to a housing shortage (Hantrais, Mangen and O'Brien, 1990). It is also unusual in having large-scale, elaborate and high quality residential facilities for people with severe disabilities. However, since the mid-1980s, there has been an increased emphasis on 'substitution': a mixing of different forms of care, including 24-hour domiciliary services and respite care, to meet the needs of users and to reduce the numbers in residential care. The effectiveness of this substitution approach is to be evaluated on the basis of evidence from six pilot projects in the early 1990s (Cohen, 1990a).

Another unusual feature of the Dutch state welfare system has been the development of occupational (or industrial) social work, whereby 1500 social workers are employed by private firms and public companies. While the employer has overall responsibility for the welfare of all employees, the provision of a social work service is mentioned in law as being important to the maintenance of good working conditions. In many situations a social worker is part of a team including a doctor and a personnel manager, and it is perhaps not surprising to note that at the training stage social workers are likely to be trained on courses in the same department as personnel managers.

Training

Most social workers belong to the National Association for Social Workers (*Landelijke Vereniging voor Maatschappelijk Werkers*), which was established in its present form in 1988. It is in the process of establishing a register to protect the use of the title 'social worker', but does not have trade union functions. Social workers are trained on four-year degree courses at *Hogenschulen* (similar to German *Fachhochschulen*) and courses include some practical work. Admission is on the basis of academic qualifications gained after five or six years of secondary education and students may follow courses leading to qualifications in either general social work, cultural work, residential work or youth welfare work (see Chapter 4).

Discussion

The foregoing illustrates some of the variety across the EC in the way social services are organised and delivered, and the national and organisational contexts within which social workers operate. It is perhaps appropriate now to try to draw out some of the similarities and differences apparent from these examples.

The role of the state in social services provision varies enormously, from having a widely accepted leading role (as in Denmark), to an acknowledged but less central position (as in Germany and Ireland), and a developing role (as in Greece and Spain). However, generally there is a *trend to increased pluralism*. There are also variations in the degree of centralisation or not, though provision of social services and employment of social workers usually rests at regional or lower levels, as in the UK. Additionally, levels of state expenditure on social services varies considerably, but a common concern has been to hold down or reduce public expenditure in the face of increasing demands. Methods of funding social service and care provisions vary from well developed insurance schemes (as in Denmark and the Netherlands) and use of money from central and local taxation (as in Spain and Germany) to a greater reliance on income from voluntary sources (as in Ireland and Germany). In relation to these last two, 'flag days', lotteries, subscriptions, welfare postage stamps, sponsorship, Church taxes and other schemes prompt individual (charitable) donations, while many countries also operate tax relief and other schemes to encourage corporate giving. Additionally, direct payment by users for services provided by the private sector already exists in relation to a (small) proportion of services, and is under further or renewed consideration in most countries.

The extent to which social workers are associated with assessment of financial need and disbursement of state money to individuals also varies, from a clear role in the process in Germany to merely an advocacy role relative to other workers in Ireland. However, it is common for provision of some financial aid to be the responsibility of the same Government department, if not of social workers themselves, and social workers generally have a closer association with this area of work than in the UK. It is also interesting to note the extent to which social work and local authority social services provision are often carried out in conjunction with health care (for example, in Greece, Germany, Ireland and the Netherlands); and it is relatively common for social workers to work to administrators or another professional group (law, medicine) outside the UK (see also Chapter 4). The Church, in most countries a traditional provider of social services, has maintained an important role in some (such as Ireland, the Netherlands and Germany) while currently playing a minimal part (as in Denmark) or having a less clear future role in others (for example, Spain and Greece). This is also true of the voluntary sector in general, although there are marked contrasts between countries where voluntary agencies are predominantly large organisations (as in Germany) and where they are more likely to be small, localised agencies (as in Ireland). Similarly, the relative importance of the private sector has changed over times in Spain, for example, but is, in most countries, being more seriously considered as a resource, as already indicated. The role of the state in approving and regulating voluntary and private agencies varies from limited (in Germany) to clear cut (in the Netherlands), though to some extent provision of financial support to some voluntary and private agencies by central or local government serves as an indicator of approval.

Turning to the informal sector, and the role of the family in particular, there is a contrast between those countries where families play an important role partly because of relative scarcity of other services (such as Greece, Spain and Ireland), and those where it has an acknowledged and continuing role, notwithstanding a relatively high level of provision of state and other services (Germany), and also those where it is seen as important but not necessarily the major provider of care for children under school age (as in Denmark) or for handicapped family members. This last is specifically the case in Denmark, where, for example, the adult status of young people with disabilities reaching the age of 18 years is fully acknowledged and carries various entitlements. The extent of small self-help/cooperative initiatives also varies, with a stronger tradition of this in some countries (Spain and Ireland) than others. Similarly, the level of consumer participation and representation varies, with this being perhaps best developed in Denmark, but also a notable feature of some Dutch and German provisions.

Turning now to the position of social work, a picture emerges of a generally youthful profession, still predominantly female, which in most countries is struggling to establish or develop its professional status. The extent to which social workers operate in uni-professional or multi-disciplinary teams varies, as does the level of professional supervision and support they can expect. Thus, for instance, Greek social workers may need to work quite independently, while Dutch social workers will expect both in-house supervision and may perhaps also pay for external consultation. Levels of unemployment also vary, although most EC countries have a surplus rather than a shortage of workers. All EC countries have a national association to which social workers can belong, but the relative strength and representiveness of these varies significantly, as do their actual role and function. Thus, at one extreme, the Danish association has union as well as professional association functions and almost all social workers in membership, and this contrasts sharply with the German situation (or indeed the British). The Spanish, Greek and Irish associations, although small and under-resourced, seem relatively representative and energetic in their support and promotion of social work at national levels. Some associations also have responsibility for regulation and registration of social workers, although elsewhere regulation is a state responsibility (for example, Spain) or not yet achieved (as in the UK).

All the national associations belong to the International Federation of Social Workers (IFSW), founded in 1956 as a successor to the International Permanent Secretariat of Social Workers originally established in Paris in 1928. This endeavours to promote the exchange of information and views, and to develop cross-country policies, including at EC level, through the European Liaison Committee. Recent concerns have included, for instance, social work responses to AIDS/HIV; cross-national adoptions; the position of elderly foreign migrants, and also of refugees and asylum seekers. In addition it is concerned about the role and status of social workers and undertakes specific studies: for example, in relation to training (the Cocozza Report, 1989) and occupational social work. Other international organisations represent particular interest groups, such as the International Association of Schools of Social Work (IASSW, founded in 1928 in Western Europe) and the International Council of Social Welfare. The latter was also founded in 1928 to promote social development. Its European region extends beyond the EC, covering 19 countries and 23 international welfare organisations. It is a non-governmental body, but has a consultative role within the Council of Europe and the EC.

With regard to the other area mentioned, namely training, this has already received attention in other studies (Brauns and Kramer, 1986; Lorenz, 1986; Barr, 1989b) and will not therefore be much expanded on here, except as it relates to mobility of social workers. The European Commission Directive of 21 December 1988 on 'a general system for recognition for higher education diplomas awarded on completion of professional education and training of at least three years duration' (effective from January 1991), has given impetus to discussion about this area (Barr, 1989a; Harris, 1990). Under this Directive cross-national mobility of professional workers must not be impeded by a national government, assuming comparability of professional training. The conditions laid down are:

1. qualifying training must be at higher education level;
2. qualifying training must be of three years' duration;
3. practice must be regulated.

Most member states meet the first two conditions in respect of social work training, and nine had reached the third by 1991, with the Italian and Portuguese national associations pressing for regulation. (The exception on both the second and third conditions is the UK.) Additionally, social workers wishing to work in another member state must demonstrate competence in language and knowledge of the relevant legislation, and can be required to undertake either an aptitude test or to undergo a period of adaptation. (This provision can also be used if the qualification falls short of that required by the host state.) Broadly speaking, social work training in the EC states has a lot of similarities. Core subjects (sociology, law, psychology, social policy, social work methods and organisation) tend to be the same, although there may be different emphases and additional subjects according to the particular course the student is taking (for example, *Sozialarbeit/Sozialpädagogik*: see Chapter 4). There are also variations in the emphasis placed on practical work (as an integrated part of the course) and the extent to which courses are seen as academic or vocational.

In fact, most training for social work, although at degree level, is carried out in tertiary level institutions which concentrate on vocational training, rather than in the university sector (with notable exceptions to this, such as Ireland). This is seen by some as contributing to the 'status problem' of social workers, and also sometimes to tensions between 'academics' who run social work training (but who may not themselves be social workers) and practitioners (as in Germany). There are also marked differences in recruitment patterns, with a bias towards students being accepted (often at 18+) on the basis of examination grades, without consideration of 'suitability' or even motivation for social work (for example, Germany and Greece). There is relatively little attempt at national planning aimed to match numbers being trained to numbers needed, though again there are exceptions (such as Denmark). It is also unusual for consideration to be given to equal opportunities issues, whether in relation to admission to higher education generally, or to the social work profession in particular. While this hardly seems to be an issue in relation to gender, it is of course in relation to class, race, age and disability; only Denmark, France and the UK seem to be promoting particular policies and schemes (including pretraining) which might address this issue (see Chapter 4). In the EC generally there is a danger that a desire for academic and professional respectability will mean that training is available only to an already privileged minority, or that it is widely available but does not lead to employment!

There are also variations in the extent to which post-qualifying training opportunities exist (or updating, re-entry or conversion courses), with relatively little development in these areas in most countries. However, there has been some development of programmes aimed at enhancing exchange and cross-national teaching and learning opportunities for social work students, at both qualifying and post-qualifying stages (Cannan, Coleman and Lyons, 1990). These are mainly under the auspices of the EC ERASMUS programme. The level of participation in these varies greatly, from the enthusiastic participation by German, Greek and Irish institutions to the relatively later involvement of Danish and Dutch schools, for instance (though student opportunities are also enhanced or limited by national policies and attainments as regards language teaching). There are also equal opportunities issues in the scheme which may be less open to mature students, women, and/or students without reasonable financial means.

Conclusion

This chapter has attempted to illustrate, through the use of selected examples, the range of national and organisational contexts within which social workers operate and to identify some of the common and contrasting elements in the role and status of social workers as a professional group, especially in relation to training. The extent to which national patterns of welfare provision and social work concerns accord with emerging EC philosophies and policies varies, as does the benefit derived from specific EC programmes, but the central themes of participation, integration and promotion of citizenship are on most national agendas at some level. Another way of developing this picture of 'European social work' is to consider the different branches of social work, and the 'client groups' or users to whom social workers relate; these will be discussed in the next chapter.

4

Branches and Themes of Social Work

Introduction

It has been indicated in the foregoing chapter that defining the field of social work practice cross-nationally is difficult, not least due to the wide range of occupational groups engaged in various forms of social work activity.

British readers, familiar with traditions of social casework, youth and community work, may look for parallels in continental Europe. However, to equate different occupational groups – *animateurs*, social pedagogues and youth workers, for instance – is to oversimplify the picture since the boundaries between training and occupational roles have considerable cross-national variations.

Given the relevance of French and German concepts in the development of branches of social work in a number of European countries, these will be examined before proceeding to present material about social work in relation to different client groups, and to identify more recently developing specialisations.

Branches of social work in France

Thevenet and Desigaux, writing in 1985 about French social work, identified three main branches within its development embracing thirteen occupational groups. (They further subdivided these according to current levels of training and functional responsibilities.) By far the largest of these branches

71

(numerically) is that including *workers concerned with the social needs of children and families*. Included within this group are *conseillères en économie social et familiale* (2800 family advisers); *aides ménagères* (65 000 family aides); as well as *assistantes de service sociale* (33 670 social workers: 1984 figures). Since 1946 a large number of these (family) social workers have been employed by agencies responsible for administration of social security benefits (*Caisses*), and their roles can include supervision of family benefits as well as monitoring of and support to families, and (increasingly) preventive social action (see Chapter 5).

The next largest branch which Thevenet and Desigaux identify is *the educative one*, and they note the existence of 27 000 *educateurs specialisés* (specialist educators) as well as four other groups in this tradition. This branch derived from a largely male occupational group involved in communal care of children in penitentiaries, *maisons de redressement* (houses of correction), orphanages and hospitals for foundlings, who developed educational approaches both to occupy the children, and to treat disturbed and/or delinquent children/youngsters unable to attend ordinary schools. This group now includes probation officers (*délégués de la liberté surveillée*) employed by the Ministry of Justice, as well as *educateurs specialisés* working with disturbed adolescents (in the residential sector), and others working to support children and young people in the community (including school and work related projects: see below).

The third branch consists of *animateurs*. These (13 600) workers come under the joint supervision of the Ministry of Social Affairs and National Solidarity and the Ministry of Free Time, Youth and Sport; they came into being at the end of the nineteenth century with the establishment of compulsory schooling and the popular education movement. They were concerned to promote access to education and leisure/cultural facilities, and since the inter-war period their work has been oriented towards young people's leisure activities. There has been a relative increase in the bases for their activities in the post-war period, especially in *maisons de jeunes et de la culture* (youth and culture centres) and more recently in *centres sociaux* (social centres) and *maisons de quartier* (community centres). This is the only group whose training and organisation is not primarily the concern of the Ministry of Social Affairs, and it is perhaps the most distinctive of the French streams, although some social pedagogues would undertake similar work in Germany, as would workers trained in *kultur Werk* (cultural work) in the Netherlands. There has been some recognition of the complexity of this situation, and at the end of the 1970s the Ministry of Social Affairs floated the idea of a single professional group (*travail social*). Developments in training at basic and post-qualifying levels during the 1980s have led to some drawing closer of different groups.

Branches of social work in Germany

In comparison the German division into only two major branches, *Sozialarbeit* (social work) and *Sozial Pädagogik* (social pedagogy) seems simpler. *Sozialarbeit*, a general social service to families and other selected groups, is one of five provisions under the Social Assistance Act (*Sozial Hilfe*) and constitutes a social work service under the auspices of the local authorities. The other provisions are allocation of funding to voluntary organisations; social (financial) assistance to clients in residential care; to clients in their own homes; and to war victims. Apart from working from the Town Hall and offering a fieldwork service to clients, these social workers are often seen as part of a remedial system, in contrast to workers trained in a pedagogic approach.

Workers trained in the social pedagogy mode in Germany (and in Denmark and the Netherlands) play a major role in the provision of services for children and young people in both community and residential settings. The first German philosopher to use the term social pedagogy (Adolph Diestenweg, 1780–1866) defined it as 'educational action by which one aims to help the poor in society'. It can be seen as a perspective, including social action, which aims to promote human welfare through child-rearing and education practices: and to prevent or ease social problems by providing people with the means to manage their own lives, and make changes in their circumstances (Hämäläinen, 1989). It can be related, perhaps, to the popular education movement as espoused by Paulo Freire, and to the educational approach put forward by Richards and Brunner as a third possibility between the (Anglo-American) polarised extremes of individual therapy and community-based political action. (Richards and Righton, 1979). It is apparent from this that the concept of pedagogy as used in Germany has a much wider meaning than in the English language, and this is true also of the French concept of *éducation*. They extend to notions of parenting, rearing and developmental support over and above the tasks of the formal education system (Ely and Stanley, 1990; Lorenz, 1991a). In Germany, workers trained in social pedagogy are often employed by local authorities and are responsible for a broad range of statutory child care responsibilities and social work with young people (*Jugendpflege*). Alternatively they may carry out youth work of a more generalised kind (*Jugendhilfe*) from a voluntary sector base, although with funding and approval from the local authorities (Lorenz, 1991a). Additionally, there is also quite a high degree of interchangeability between people trained in different approaches (*sozialarbeit/pädagogik*) but taking up the same type of posts and, as previously mentioned, a common foundation year in training (*Sozial Wegen*) has already been established for both groups.

Services for traditional client groups

Children and families

As already indicated, concerns about family poverty and care of children have deep roots in many European countries, and work with these clients groups is universal throughout the EC. It can be conveniently divided into (preventive) work with families in the community; child protection; fostering and adoption; and residential child-care. Some information will be given about each of these areas.

National respondents to a small-scale survey carried out by one of the writers in 1990 all describe work with *children and families* as being the responsibility of social workers employed by the state. There is some evidence to suggest that in France, Germany and Italy the association between financial provision and social work is currently resulting in high case loads and bureaucratic pressures limiting the amount of time which social workers can give to family work, including preventive work (Cigno, 1985; F. Hooper, 1987; Henderson and Scott, 1988). Undoubtedly the close working knowledge which this gives social workers of the needs of poor families and the impact of government policies equips them to act as advocates for this group, but this assumes political skills and a degree of organisation and representation on the part of social workers themselves (for example, through a professional association or specific lobbying groups). An additional possibility is the development of more educational and power-sharing modes of work with families in local communities, as developed through decentralised 'patch' projects, and there has been some development in this direction in most countries, sometimes from health centre bases (as in Italy, Greece and Ireland), sometimes from social centres and local offices (as in France: see Chapter 5), and sometimes from patch offices or community centres on particular estates.

An example of the last can be given from Germany (Koblenz, Rhineland Pfalz) where the municipal authority funded a worker (under the auspices of CARITAS) to establish a patch office in a flat on an estate built in the 1950s and offering low-rent, relatively poor-quality housing to 300 families (15 per cent gypsy, 23 per cent Turkish, and a high proportion of East Europeans). This estate had relatively large proportions of single-parent families, unemployed people and children attending the local school for children with special needs; residents experienced a sense of isolation and discrimination both within and outside the estate. Over a 10-year period projects have been developed which address a range of needs: stimulation of the estate's pre-school children; a place to do homework and relax out of school for older children; activities for young people; and a place to meet, relax and become involved in community activities for parents. By the mid-1980s a new community centre had been established, partly with money raised by an annual community festival, and attention was being turned to the needs of the estate's elderly residents and to the upgrading of the physical fabric of the estate itself.

There are also, of course, *specialist facilities* for work with children and families in virtually all EC countries, often developed by the voluntary sector or in conjunction with multi-disciplinary teams in health (psychiatric) settings. Organisations such as *Pro Familia* (Germany) provide counselling services to pregnant women, couples in conflict, and parents with child-rearing concerns, while Martin Textor has described the development (also in Germany) of *Sozial Pädagogische Familienhilfe* (social–educational family help) since 1969. This approach offers an intensive form of social work intervention (10–20 hours per week over a 1–3-year period) to individual families 'who cannot be reached by counselling agencies or traditional social work'. This work, undertaken by 2000 staff (with varied training), and financed by Youth Welfare Departments, is now offered in about half the (former West) German authorities (Textor, 1990).

Child protection. A major challenge facing social work in most EC countries has been the (re-) emergence of concern about child protection. While a survey of national associations carried out by the British Association of Social Workers (BASW) in the early 1980s produced a very low response rate, suggesting that this was predominantly a British problem, by the end of the decade evidence showed that it was becoming a major concern and priority for social work in the majority of EC states.

In Ireland an embargo on new social work appointments to health authorities had to be lifted in the late 1980s in recognition of pressure workers were under in this area of work (*IFSW Newsletter*, April 1988), which is also shared with the Irish Society for the Prevention of Cruelty to Children; and, in Germany, while study visits by student groups in the early 1980s found no evidence of concern about this problem, by 1989 both staff employed by the Youth Welfare Department and voluntary sector specialist agencies included discussion of this aspect of their work in presentations. In France social workers' concerns about rising referral rates led to their national association (ANAS), producing a special edition of their journal on this topic in 1990 (*La Revue Française de Service Social*, No. 157/158, 1990).

Although there are no comprehensive data yet on the relative incidence of the problem, and the level of public awareness varies considerably, all EC member states now have legislation and resources related to this issue, and some systems (such as the Danish) include mandatory reporting (Davies and Sale, 1989). A study of these systems reveals interesting differences in the extent to which emphasis is placed on preventive community-based strategies, and help provided to families on a voluntary basis, relative to statutory intervention and concern with separation of the child from the offending parent(s). It also shows up variations in the extent to which different professional groups are expected (or required) to work together, and different patterns of relationships between social workers and the medical and legal professions in particular. While there is not space to detail particular systems here, it is perhaps interesting to note that in the Netherlands social workers are far more likely to work to doctors as part of the confidential doctor system (initial referral and assessment) or in the Department of Justice (if legal action may be necessary), while in France social workers from a variety of agencies may be involved at the initial stages and on a voluntary basis, but a major role is taken by social workers in the Ministry of Justice working to Children's Judges (Ely and Stanley, 1990).

Alternative care. Turning to *fostering and adoption*, both these areas have relatively long traditions as areas of social work responsibility. As in the UK, much of the development in other European countries stems from work by voluntary organisations, and in Greece, for instance, adoption continues to be primarily the responsibility of two particular voluntary agencies (with some informal/illegal adoption still taking place). Similarly, development of fostering has been a relatively late alternative to residential care for children, and is as yet fairly limited in the Mediterranean countries or in Ireland, where pressure of other work prevents processing of applications from prospective foster parents (J. King, 1990b). In most northern European countries, residential care for children is generally now seen as a specialist resource for a limited few, and more emphasis has been put on fostering, resulting in a decline in adoption consequent on reduced birth rates and public acceptance of different family patterns.

To give a national example, in (former West) Germany adoptions are carried out through the Youth Welfare Departments, and in 1990 there were about 3000 adoptions per annum, relative to about 30 000 requests. About half the children needing alternative care are now placed in foster homes (also by youth officers), and this can be higher in some areas (for instance in Koblenz, 160 children were in care, and 140 were in foster homes in 1985). Applicants have to be assessed (clinical, medical, hygiene and accommodation factors) and may be offered pre-fostering training and post-fostering support, although both are variable. Fostering arrangements are flexible and may include day care and 5-day week arrangements as well as 24-hour, longer-term placements. Young people leaving foster homes usually have the offer of subsidised accommodation from the Youth Welfare Office.

The picture concerning *residential care* for children as already indicated is similarly varied: provisions range from relatively large and traditionally run orphanages for children in Greece, through some surprisingly large facilities for children in Germany and the Netherlands (invariably run by voluntary organisations) to small-scale establishments in Denmark. However, this is an area of change. In Greece a resolution has recently been passed that orphanages should be closed and foster care developed, and in Germany and also the Netherlands and Belgium the size of residential establishments is under review with a move to smaller-scale homes already occurring, or likely to (Colton *et al.*, 1991). To give an example from Germany, this has meant a reduction from 600 boys in one home to 120. The home was initially set up by CARITAS, but its governing body now includes 50 per cent representation from local authorities. Fees are charged and paid by local authorities. Boys aged over 7 years can be referred if their care or education is lacking and/or as a result of offending behaviour, and, further, if social work intervention with the family has proved ineffective. The home has little control over admissions, although these are discussed between the social or youth worker, a teacher representative of the home and the parent(s). Boys can be admitted on a court order or by agreement with the parent(s), and there is a secure unit which can take up to five boys for a time-limited period (usually 3–6 months).

Most boys there have educational problems (learning difficulties, non-attendance), as well as social problems. The aim of the home is to promote personal, social and educational development and to provide vocational training for older youths. Boys attend classes in the morning and have recreation, homework and/or vocational training in the afternoons. The boys live in eleven groups of 12 in mixed-age flats around the main building (with its educational, vocational and recreational facilities) and are cared for by four care staff (not usually trained in *sozialarbeit* or *pädagogik*, although they may hold other qualifications). There is also a special group for the oldest youths (up to 20 years) and self-catering flats for those near to leaving. Boys stay on average about three years, and there are provisions for home visits (a 2-week annual holiday and one weekend a month) and visits by parents. Absconders may be brought before/returned to the court and may face prison if aged over 14. The staff total of 120 includes twelve teachers, two speech therapists, a psychologist, care assistants and domestics. Plans for discharge and aftercare are made with social/youth workers from the boy's home area. Apparently, this home for boys (in Rhineland Pfalz) is not unusual in size, and indeed another institution, with 140 places was visited on another occasion. This catered for 7–19-year-olds (90 per cent of them boys), of whom only a proportion were fully resident, some being fostered with couples locally while others lived with their own families and attended the school facilities on a daily basis.

This model and scale of care can be contrasted with two examples from Denmark, one a residential home for 24 children aged 6–15 years with emotional and social problems, and the other a unit for 25 children (aged 2–18 years) who had been sexually abused. In the first the predominantly social work staff had been trained in family therapy techniques, and in the second in social pedagogic techniques; in both the emphasis was on care, treatment and reintegration into family and community rather than on education and training.

Young people

Turning now more specifically to young people, this is another group which receives social work provision by either specially trained youth workers or (generic) social workers in all European countries, either through statutory or voluntary agencies.

In Luxembourg services for young people are provided by the Ministry of Education and relate mainly to young people with a physical or mental disability or those who have come before the courts (Munday, 1990), while in Belgium at least part of the social work services available to young people are delivered through the *school system*. Multi-disciplinary school guidance teams include (school) social workers, who are formally employed by the Ministry of Education and have a statutory basis for their work. School social workers are based on-site in ordinary and special schools, are available to children and young people aged 3–18 years, and are particularly concerned with pupils with social problems resulting in non-attendance or unhappiness and poor performance in the school environment. School social work is also reported to be a feature of wider social work provision in Greece, Netherlands and Spain, although only on a small scale, and also exists in France and Germany. In the two latter countries social workers trained in the educative tradition are particularly likely to be involved in helping young people with school problems or in providing generally available out-of-school activities. Grossman (1988) described the development of up to about 30 school-based social work projects (aimed at developing the school environment as a more positive experience for young people) in (former West) Germany since the late 1960s. The main tasks of such workers are to provide small-scale 'contact' places, where homework can be completed and attention given to the social and emotional needs of (secondary-school-age) pupils. Group work, individual counselling and recreational opportunities are offered, and the school social worker liaises with school staff, parents, vocational advisers, and youth welfare workers as appropriate.

Apart from school-based social work, *éducateurs* in France and employees of the *Jugendamt* (Youth Welfare Department) in Germany have duties to develop *leisure services* for young people, to offer social and educational day and residential programmes, to protect young people (including in family and employment situations), and may also undertake detached youth work or set up projects for young people with particular problems (homelessness, drugs, unemployment). The 9th Plan of the French Ministry of Social Affairs (1984–8) identified *l'insertion sociale des jeunes 16–25* (that is, integration into community and employment) as one of its priorities along with *la prévention sociale*, prevention of juvenile maladjustment and delinquency through leisure and training opportunities, especially over the holiday periods (M. King, 1988).

Concerns about alienation and deviance among young people motivate some provisions as much as welfare considerations, and youth officers interviewed in a small town in Germany (Rhineland Pfalz) referred to the sense of pressure and stigma they experience in their work, partly because of their powers (to remove children and young people at risk in their families) and partly because of the expectations placed on them of being able to cure problems of drug, alcohol and solvent abuse and football hooliganism among disaffected and often unemployed young people. Staff work a 40-hour week, spending about 20 per cent of their time doing youth and group work in a community centre, and the remainder on case work, each youth officer having an average monthly workload of about 50 cases. They see the need for more developmental/preventive work, and also work to improve liaison and relations with local voluntary organisations, but feel constrained by current responsibilities and workloads. At the time of writing it remains to be seen how the implementation of the 1991 (German) Children and Young Persons Act might affect this situation (Lorenz, 1991b).

Social work intervention in response to *juvenile delinquency* is a well established area of work (usually carried out separately from work with adult offenders). Thus, youth workers from the *Jugendamt* in Germany may submit court reports on juveniles, and also may run schemes for young offenders referred by probation officers (similar to intermediate treatment in the UK). One such scheme in Koblenz, which started in the late 1970s initially as a student project with funding from CARITAS, has since been taken over by the *Jugendamt* with funding also from the Ministry of Justice. It is now one of about 50 such schemes in Germany, and provides a 3-month programme of weekly group meetings and two residential weekends for 10 young offenders (aged 14–21 years). Each programme is planned in conjunction with the group, and includes advice and informal sessions, leisure activities and video work on their offending behaviour. Contracts are made with group members about attendance and behaviour in the group, and failure to comply may result in being returned to court (by the probation officer) and committed to prison.

Adult offenders

This leads on to consideration of work with adult offenders. While all respondents indicated some provisions for social work with offenders this is usually provided by separate (probation) departments accountable to a different Ministry (such as the Ministry of Justice in France) and, apart from Ireland, areas of responsibility may not be the same as those of probation departments in the UK. A particular difference is the exclusion of matrimonial and domestic proceedings from probation officers' responsibilities (for example, in the Netherlands and Germany), although there may be other areas of similarity, such as the development of community services schemes in the Netherlands and Denmark. A visit to a probation office in Koblenz, Germany, elicited the following information. Probation orders constitute a sentence, and can be made consequent upon or concurrent with custodial sentences (actual or suspended). Probation officers must agree to accept the offender, and the probationer has to sign to accept conditions of probation and acknowledge consequences of breaking the conditions (that is, returning to court and likely imprisonment). Usual conditions would concern residence; school or work attendance; contact with the probation officer; and may include restitution to the victim or, for example, to the Red Cross. Probation officers have to submit monthly progress reports to the court and orders may run for 1–4 years, (for juveniles aged over 14) or 2–5 years (for adults aged over 18–20, depending on 'social and moral maturity'). The office in Koblenz consists of 18 officers (for a population of 1.3 million people), and each officer carries 70–80 cases at a time. One officer has overall responsibility, but otherwise the system lacks a hierarchical structure or addition of assistants.

People with physical or mental disabilities

Provision for people with physical and/or mental disabilities is most likely to be made through domiciliary, day care or residential services provided by agencies in the voluntary sector, although most EC states provide some form of public financial assistance to adults with disabilities, and in some cases subsidise services provided by the voluntary sector (as in France, Germany, the Netherlands and Denmark) in accordance with principles of choice and subsidiarity. In the Netherlands, current concern about the large number of disabled people dependent on state benefits is resulting in attempts to integrate more disabled people into paid work in the public and private sectors. A recent trend towards putting increased resources into domiciliary care indicates a move away from a well-established tradition of residential care for people with disabilities. This provision has often been of a high standard, on a large scale (up to 1000 residents and catering for a wide age range, from 5 to 80 years), although again recent policy changes suggest a reduction in scale, perhaps to homes for 200 people (Cohen, 1990a). It is also recognised that a move to care in the community will lead to an increase in demand for places in sheltered workshops, and may lead to less availability in specialist equipment and social work expertise. (Social workers are employed in some of the large institutions, working mainly with the families of residents.) However, consumer groups, such as *Gehandicappen Raad* (an organisation for disabled people), are trying to ensure that the needs and interests of disabled people themselves are respected. In Denmark, similar concerns over the loss of specialist resources and expertise which can be found in large-scale organisations occurred in 1988, when services for people with disabilities were devolved from 14 regional authorities to 275 local authorities, who now sometimes sub-contract responsibility for these provisions to the voluntary or private sectors.

Another interesting feature (for British readers) noted in both Dutch and German provisions is the mixing of age and disability groups. For example, in Germany such mixed centres are run on a regional basis by the National Association for Disabled People (which grew out of the Parents' Association for Cerebral Palsy, established in the 1960s) for a potential population of 1.5 million. While this is not one of the Big Six voluntary organisations, it does receive some state funding as well as drawing on parental contributions, donations and the results of fund-raising activities. A typical centre is staffed on an interdisciplinary basis (with medical, psychological and social work staff augmenting the work of care assistants) and includes a kindergarten; a day centre for severely disabled adults; and assessment and treatment provisions for children. The kindergarten can take up to 75 children in seven groups of 3–6-year-olds. Referrals come from local doctors or can be made from ordinary kindergartens if specialist assessment is needed. The centre staff can offer diagnosis, speech therapy and play therapy, and they work with parents to identify future needs and plans. At 6 years old most children will transfer to a special school in the region which they can attend until aged 19 years. If it is not possible for young adults to take up a place in a sheltered workshop they may then be referred back to the centre for one of the 35 places (in six groups) in the day centre. The overall aims of the centre are to promote the independence of children and adults with a disability as far as possible, but also to provide relief and support to the families. To this end additional services, such as holidays for children, respite care, occasional day and weekend programmes in the school holidays, and a baby-sitting service are offered. Social workers also undertake groupwork sessions with parents and siblings, and parents can receive genetic counselling. Families are actively involved in the management of the centre through the Parents' Board, which meets monthly, and can contribute directly to the running of the centre through voluntary work alongside the staff.

Mentally ill people

The nineteenth-century institutionalisation and late twentieth-century decarceration of mentally ill people took place across Europe. Despite a relatively well-established stream of psychiatric social work in most Northern European countries (often drawing on North American models) this client group seems relatively less well catered for by community social work services than others, particularly in the Mediterranean countries. A small number of community mental health projects and centres are gradually being established in Spain and Greece, and notably in Italy (the latter in response to a mass closure of psychiatric hospitals in the 1970s) but psychiatric problems generally still tend to be medicalised, often because of the insurance system, and seen as needing medical treatment and care sometimes provided by the private sector through medical insurance, as in Germany and France (Mangen, 1985; K. Jones, 1988). There has been some development in provisions for this group in Germany since the mid-1970s, partly resulting from the establishment of consumer groups articulating needs, and operating as mutual-support groups (as with MIND in the UK); and partly as a result of a major report, critical of psychiatric hospitals, at that time.

One such provision has been the growth of half-way houses or hostels for ex-psychiatric patients (established under the auspices of the Ministry of Health); there are now three in the Rhineland Pfalz region, for example, (funded by the

Land but run by one of the Big Six voluntary organisations).
Typically, they accommodate between 20 and 30 people (male
and female, aged 18–50 years), for up to about 18 months.
During this time residents live communally (in subgroups),
and are responsible for their own shopping, cooking and
cleaning. Some take up paid employment, or places are
sought in sheltered workshops. Most residents are on medi-
cation, and they are supervised and assisted by a small team
of social workers and perhaps a psycho-therapist. Weekly
group meetings are held, and social skills training, and training for work is given. One worker undertakes outreach/
support work with residents who have moved on. Funding is
now being sought to subsidise flats for independent living. It
is estimated that 10 per cent of psychiatric patients in Germany have passed through hostels over the past decade, and
15 per cent have returned to families. A further 10 per cent
are long-stay patients, and the remainder are discharged to
live in the community (though it is not known what the re-
admission rates are).

Older people

Care for frail or destitute older people has a long tradition in
Europe, mostly in the informal sector (relatives, neighbours)
or through the Church (such as the St Vincent de Paul
Society). This is still reflected in a large proportion of services for older people, whether community-based or residential, being provided through the voluntary sector, with or
without state funding (see below). Although all EC states
make some financial provisions (pensions, assistance) for
elderly residents this varies widely, resulting in a proposal in
the Social Charter that there should be a minimum income
plus some social and medical assistance as a right for all EC
elderly people.

Turning to some national examples of care for elderly, it
should also be noted that attitudes to family responsibility
and residential care for elderly people varies. Thus in Greece
there are still high expectations that elders should be cared
for at home by their families, reflected in low levels of domi-

ciliary services (available to only 0.5 per cent of the elderly population) and of residential care (0.4 per cent: see A. Jamieson in Hantrais, Mangen and O'Brien, 1990). Meanwhile, in both Italy and Spain, slightly more opportunities for residential care exist (Italy has 1.5 per cent of elderly people in residential care), and there is no stigma in seeking such services. Indeed Spanish homes, which are often large (500 residents) and run by the state (having been taken over from the voluntary sector), may have long waiting lists and admit relatively able-bodied residents from perhaps overcrowded family homes. However, there are also smaller homes, including ones still in the voluntary or private sector, and these may be more comparable with nursing homes, with a higher proportion of residents experiencing disability or dementia (Eaton, 1990a). Charges for care are met from individual state pensions (30 per cent) supplemented by local municipal funding, and there is a growing concern to define admissions policies more clearly so that places are allocated to the most needy.

The use of residential care to ease overcrowding at home is seen most strongly in the Netherlands, which has the highest proportion of people aged over 65 in residential care in the EC (12 per cent relative to the next highest, Denmark, at 6 per cent; Hantrais, Mangen and O'Brien, 1990). While residential care provided by the voluntary and private sector with some state funding is of a good standard, and again often on quite a large scale, there have been moves since the late 1980s to reduce the size of residential establishments, the scale of provision and the huge waiting lists for care. Initial results from pilot projects in support of this new policy (dynamic substitution) suggested that 40 per cent of people could manage in their own homes, particularly if extra domiciliary services were available, and projects are now continuing to develop small-scale residential, day care and domiciliary services integrated into local communities. Interesting features of the Dutch system are the inclusion of social workers in assessment committees for residential care, and in the newer developments; and also the representation of older people's groups in policy-making and resource allocation forums (Cohen, 1990b).

The Dutch tradition of residential care can be contrasted with France, which has a longstanding policy of caring for older people in their own homes (although 5 per cent of people over 65 are in residential care). Approximately 80 per cent of these services are provided by the voluntary sector via *conventions* (agreements) with the *départements* (regional centres of authority). These can be either technical (where the voluntary agency has its own resource and staff) or financial (where the *département* provides funding and possibly also staff). Funding also comes from various *régimes* (occupationally-based insurance schemes) and this tends to create both a complex and inequitable system, since individuals within the same locality may be entitled to more or fewer services according to the policies of their *régimes* rather than according to need. The picture is further complicated by differential funding according to age, illness or disability of the client, although these may be interrelated. Local communities can undertake some direct service provision, assuming they establish themselves as a voluntary organisation and agree a *convention* with the local authority, and there is an umbrella organisation called UNASSAD (*L' Union Nationale des Associations de Soins et Services à Domicile*) for agencies which provide care at home for older people (Bartlett, 1989).

A final point in relation to needs and provisions for older people is an increasing concern with the plight of the migrant elderly, predominantly from Britain, Denmark, the Netherlands and Germany, who have retired to (often purpose-built) homes in Spain and, to a lesser extent, Portugal. There are now 75 000 such residents in the Costa Blanca region of Spain (total population 1.2 million) and problems can arise if either their financial resources do not meet the (higher than anticipated) cost of living or if their health (physical or mental) deteriorates. Although these populations can draw their national pensions and are entitled to Spanish health care (under EC reciprocal arrangements), the Spanish medical services place reliance on family support for patients in hospital, and this may be lacking for elderly migrants. Problems are often compounded by lack of fluency in Spanish on the part of elderly migrants, and the limited availability of social services (Eaton, 1990d). National groups have tended to set up their own self-help systems (such as HELP, a British support network run by volunteers), and Spanish delegates raised the issue with EC ministers at an IFSW meeting in 1990 as one which needs attention at the European policy level. This is one of a number of new areas of social concern with implication for policy and social work practice which will now be discussed.

New developments in social work and social services

The above comments highlight a new concern of a pan-European nature, that of migrant populations, which has other aspects which shall be addressed later. However, it is also the case that new developments are taking place in individual countries, which are sometimes paralleled elsewhere but not necessarily, and some brief examples follow.

Some national examples

Occupational social work is a well-established area of practice in some countries (such as France and the Netherlands), but has only recently begun to develop elsewhere. For example, a recent directive by the Greek Ministry of Labour stipulated that all factories over a certain size should employ a nurse and a social worker. While not required by law (and not an entirely new phenomenon), the appointment of social workers to a number of companies in Ireland has also taken place in the last decade. This development was initiated in American-owned companies, but a higher proportion are now to be found in indigenous companies. Greece has also identified social work appointments to the military as a new development; and Ireland has noted the establishment of a small hospice movement, including social work appointments (as distinct from a long tradition of care for the dying by the Poor Clare Sisters). The response to concern about increase in Aids and HIV positive cases has been patchy, with most countries seeing this as an area requiring medical intervention, sometimes supplemented by self-help and voluntary-sector initiatives, and/or by counselling provided by psychologists. Similarly, responses to people with drug or alcohol problems, while increasingly identified as social problems and sometimes attracting Government funding for projects, tend to be from the self-help and voluntary sectors rather than social workers in the statutory services. However, some counselling for drug addicts apparently takes place from social service centres in Spain (Munday, 1989); and the national association representing social workers in Denmark has been urging the Government to increase resources available for services to this group (*IFSW Newsletter*, November 1990). Problems of homelessness are also on the increase, although the causes (family violence, addiction, poverty, institutionalisation) and client groups affected are varied, resulting in a range of provisions usually under the auspices of the voluntary sector, such as the Simon Community (Ireland) and St Vincent de Paul (Ireland and France); however, night shelters and emergency accommodation are often state-funded (as in Italy and France).

Ethnic minorities and refugees

As indicated in Chapter 2, an area of increasing concern throughout the EC relates to the plight of non-EC nationals. Such people may be political refugees or asylum-seekers; or people who have migrated recently or even some time ago for economic reasons. Obviously their needs and national responses to them may be different, but virtually every EC country now has an area of social work and/or social services provision related to the needs of an estimated 15 million third-country nationals who live permanently in EC states (Flynn, 1989), and/or people seeking refugee status.

Programmes for non-EC nationals tend to be of two types: (a) emergency provisions for individuals and groups who have arrived as refugees; and (b) specific services aimed at established (and sometimes second-generation) ethnic minorities whose needs were initially primarily economic. A possible third area of specialist provision exists in some countries in relation to 'travellers' (Ireland) or *gitanos* (Spain: see

Eaton, 1990b). In relation to refugees, the Netherlands, Spain, Greece, Italy, Denmark, (West) Germany, France and the UK all have some provisions, although these vary from informal networks of self-help groups, through reception centres (often run by voluntary agencies with or without state funding), to longer-term camps where basic services, some language tuition and social work assistance aimed at resettlement may be provided.

The problems of economic migrants vary from those of the newly arrived to those of the long established. In the case of the former their problems may be similar to those of refugees: they may have difficulties with language; with obtaining work permits and/or work; with establishing legal entitlement to residential status and welfare services; and in maintaining their dependents at home or making provision for them to join them.

Specific organisations and programmes may attempt to meet some of these needs. However, such groups may also be particularly vulnerable to economic or political changes at national or international level. One such example were the 100 000 or so Moroccans in Spain, who found themselves liable to arrest and deportation without appeal, at the time of Gulf War in 1991 (specifically because of their Muslim connections, but made more vulnerable by widespread problems in gaining legal entry, documents, and rights to residence and work: see J. Hooper, 1991).

In relation to longer established ethnic minorities, self-help and mutual aid initiatives may be augmented by the formal establishment of projects under the auspices of voluntary organisations catering for the needs of specific groups, and for the acceptance by the state of responsibilities in relation to particular communities (though this may be mainly through the voluntary sector). Thus in Germany, for example, the welfare needs of 900 ethnic minority workers and their families in Koblenz have been divided up primarily according to ethnicity, and services are provided by separate voluntary agencies (the *Arbeiterwohlfahrt* relates mainly to Turkish and Moroccan communities; *Diakonischeswerk* to the boat people and Greek communities; and CARITAS provides services mainly for Catholic groups). Many of these groups are well established (50 per cent of all migrant workers in what used to be West Germany had been in the country for more than 15 years by 1990, and two-thirds for more than 10 years), so services often relate to the needs of children and young people – particularly with reference to maintaining their cultural traditions and identity – while also aiming at assisting integration and improving their opportunities and status.

One such project is a German-Turkish centre, located in a building donated by the city, but whose running and funding are the responsibility of the voluntary organisation and local community. This centre houses kindergarten facilities for local Turkish and German pre-school children (and includes a Turkish worker who does some separate sessions with the Turkish children): and also serves as a community and adult-education centre for young people and adults. It provides both German and Turkish language classes (the latter aimed at local teachers and other professionals who might be working with the Turkish community), and also sewing, cooking, handicrafts and vocational education activities, including developing a local newspaper. It is staffed by two paid workers, volunteers, and students undertaking project work. It has operated primarily as a cultural centre for the Turkish population rather than a focus for genuine interchange between Turkish and German people, and also has attracted women and children, rather than Turkish males (whose social life tends to be more focused on bars and social clubs); as with similar projects of this kind, there are periodic concerns about whether this is a provision for the Turkish community (meeting assumed needs) or a centre in which the users themselves determine needs and services.

An area of increasing concern in a number of EC states is the work prospects of young, second-generation immigrants. In some respects this is part of a wider concern about poverty and unemployment, including youth unemployment (already discussed, but see also Chapter 5), and it was another concern voiced to EC ministers at an IFSW delegates' meeting in April 1990. However, there are also specific programmes aiming both to increase the opportunities of young people, and to train more people equipped to work with particular ethnic minority communities. Thus, in 1984, the French Ministry of Social Affairs established a special programme aimed at training disadvantaged young people (particularly Algerian, Moroccan, Tunisian and Spanish nationals) to become *animateurs*. The plan was to offer 300 places on 15 courses to be developed at appropriate centres throughout the country, and to offer grants at the minimum wage level for students to take a 3-year programme. However, as with a similar scheme promoted more recently in the UK (Youth and Community Work Apprenticeship Scheme), there have been some problems with low take-up.

Overall, there is a general indication that at national and EC levels efforts are being made to restrict immigration for whatever reason, and two groups in particular are working on immigration controls. The first of these, the Trevi group, is an informal coordinating group of EC Home Offices (Ministers and civil servants) concerned with combating terrorism, drug trafficking and illegal immigration. The second is the Schengen Group, a treaty organisation consisting of Germany, France, Belgium, the Netherlands and Luxembourg, which is developing a common immigration policy related to removal of internal border controls. Thus there is concern first that refusal of an entry visa by one country will automatically make an applicant *persona non grata* by other signatories of the Treaty; second, that the opportunities of free movement within the Community will be a right of the white citizens of member states, but of doubtful value to those identified by skin colour as immigrants; and third, that all ethnic minorities will be more vulnerable to checks on their status in a wider range of situations (such as health care, job or housing applications) than at present.

Conclusion

This chapter has tried to clarify some of the similarities and differences between the main branches of social work, as represented by French and German traditions, and to give some illustrative examples of social work practice with, and provisions for, a range of client groups.

Some common themes can be identified, such as pressures on statutory social workers from large caseloads and bureaucratic procedures; the tension between providing services which the state requires or professionals determine, relative to promoting more community-based, consumer-led approaches; and pressure to establish community care schemes and limit the use of residential care. We also indicated some new areas of work, either identified by specific countries or arising from common concerns within the EC. Some of these could be exacerbated by increased (EC) labour mobility or by wider and less predictable population movements related to international political and economic tensions.

Thus, concern about comparability of child-care policies, procedures and standards; about the possible increase in mobility of older people or people with mental health problems or other vulnerabilities; and about the rights and opportunities of people from ethnic minorities, are likely to require EC (rather than just national) responses. Already, networks are developing which aim to protect or promote the interests of particular groups; and increasingly policies and programmes are being devised at EC level which have an impact on national conditions. These will be more specifically considered in Chapter 6, after we focus in the next chapter on changes in French social work and their relevance to debates on citizenship, and the development of social work in an EC context.

5

A People's Europe?
French Social Workers and
Les Exclus

'A people's Europe should be a Europe of solidarity,
especially as regards the most underprivileged.'
(Commission of the EC, April 1987).

Social action: from clients to citizens

The appearance of new forms of poverty (or the rediscovery
of poverty: see Chapter 2) in the 1970s and 1980s has provoked a debate on the welfare state (*l'État-Providence*) and *les
exclus*. Traditional social work and social assistance seemed
to perpetuate the dependency and marginalisation of the
disadvantaged; indeed, it seemed to be a mechanism of exclusion (Thevenet and Desigaux, 1985). At the same time
the costs of the welfare state were increasing and, faced with
rising unemployment and limits to economic growth, the
French Socialist government of 1981–6 challenged social
workers, youth workers, the police, those in the fields of
sport and leisure and local politicians to work together to
find ways of preventing crime, delinquency and exclusion
(M. King, 1988). The 1982–3 decentralisation of many areas
of government has given further impetus to this collaboration and partnership, and to the challenge to create imaginative social strategies at the local level. The 9th Plan (1984–8)
emphasised the social development of neighbourhoods and
action aimed at groups rather than individuals: for instance,

the struggle against drug abuse, measures in favour of immigrants, and the social integration of young people between 16 and 25. Social action, then, means an emphasis on finding new ways of working with groups, especially those on the margins. Social work is now involved in the search for new forms of social protection, which integrate rather than exclude, which validate users as such, or as workers, or as members of social groups, rather than stigmatising them as 'clients'.

The revitalisation of 'degraded' neighbourhoods is a cornerstone in preventive social action; it combines the physical renovation of rundown estates or inner city areas with the (re)creation of employment and of community – *voisinage* – and thus bonds of solidarity. A key concept is that of *insertion*, or integration, which can be understood either in economic (employment) terms or socially, as membership of groups such as the family or association. This form of social action is influential in EC social policy (for instance, in the current ELISE poverty programme: see Chapter 1); it rests upon a French notion of 'the social': the sphere of social problems and its relationship with the organisation of society. Concepts of social rights, of citizenship and of solidarity are connected to a vision of the totality of society as much as to the needs of particular groups or individuals. The principle of solidarity is unfamiliar in British social policy in its emphasis on the importance of group cohesion, and collective action on behalf of the wider society (see Chapter 2 for a fuller discussion).

It is notable that the contemporary French conception of solidarity focuses on the dangers to society of exclusion, and that it seeks ways of raising the status of 'clients' to that of users who participate alongside non-stigmatised users and are valorised by their involvement and participation in social networks and provision. Social work, then, is facing the major challenge of drawing *les exclus* into the mainstream, and of working across a wide range of social groups in so doing. This has provoked debates within the profession as to the significance of this for social work's autonomy, values, accountability and mandate. This chapter will look at these recent changes in French social work practice and at the dilemmas for social work, focusing on unemployment and then on child care, and will conclude with a discussion of citizenship.

Social action and unemployment

Revenu Minimum d'Insertion

The *Revenu Minimum d'Insertion* (RMI) is a new financial benefits and an ambitious scheme established by President Mitterrand in 1988 with the aim of preventing the exclusion and personal decline of the long-term unemployed, of the 'new poor', as well as of finding ways to renovate the welfare state. French social security is based on an insurance system; those who fall into long-term unemployment and those who have not yet found work have until now had only an erratic safety net. The consequences of unemployment – homelessness, crime and exclusion of youth (in short, an underclass) – were perceived as growing risks to society. Now those who join the RMI (RMistes) have a right and an obligation to engage in training or education (often of an informal kind) or in various forms of community work, specifically designed to meet their needs and capabilities. Social workers are heavily involved in making assessments, drawing up the contracts and following the agreed *insertion* activities.

This programme has had two important consequences: first, it has given claimants and users more status and emphasised their autonomy rather than dependence; second, it has drawn social workers into local partnership under the umbrella of the *Commission locale d'insertion* (CLI). Social work has been given a high profile by the government: Michel Rocard (as Prime Minister) and the Minister of Solidarity both urged social workers during the hugely publicised launch of the RMI to attack social exclusion, and said that the success of the project depended upon them. The law setting out the new provisions received remarkably unanimous support. Rocard presented it as a revolution in welfare entitlement, a massive new initiative in meeting the challenge of inequality and deprivation and in avoiding the lower level of citizenship implied by traditional social assistance. *Insertion* is the route to solidarity:

> The use of the word 'insertion' is in itself interesting and instructive: poor and disadvantaged people are seen as being excluded from Society, rejected by it, and the purpose of such policy initiatives is to bring them back within it. Hence the new benefit is seen as a 'tool of social transformation', not an element in a policy of social assistance. Perhaps 'rehabilitation' is the nearest English equivalent, although the less familiar term 'habilitation' is more accurate, since it does not imply that the person concerned had at some previous time been a full member of society. (Collins, 1990, 120–1)

The project encourages imaginative and locally devised solutions. While RMI is new, it is based on pre-existing smaller guaranteed income schemes for the uninsured or underinsured poor which were developed in some cities in the early 1980s. These had introduced beneficiaries to the world of work often of a voluntary kind (Connock, 1987; Collins, 1990). Social workers have for some time been working within these schemes which straddle the world of unemployment and *insertion*. How have they viewed this work?

There have been positive and negative reactions: the 'negatives' express concern about an increasing potential for surveillance and social control, about the increasing workload and loss of autonomy, and about the government's unrealistic expectations of social work. The 'positives' argue that the social action mission strengthens social work, and legitimises and broadens social work's valorisation of *les exclus*, as well as commitment to the quality of life and human rights.

Let us begin with the positives. First, we should note that the programme itself has had an impact on the environment of social work: new posts and projects have been created in the employment and training fields (especially for youth), and there are parallel schemes in the renovation of housing and inner cities and in delinquency and crime prevention, which give a framework of optimism, growth and collaboration. While social work has always seen its mission as promoting the social integration (or rehabilitation) of its clients, it is now working in more public, accountable ways, and with a broader clientele. Guyard, director of the voluntary agency *La Sauvegarde de l'Adolescence* in Paris, argues: 'Indirectly the struggle against unemployment has become a form of social action, a priority for local professionals' (*les professionels du secteur*: Guyard, 1988, p. 98).

She goes on to argue that teams of social workers therefore need to develop their competence and skills in working at all levels in the labour market. Social workers need to be well informed on all the types of training, job opportunities and employment initiatives available in their areas, connecting the *insertion* of employment with social *insertion* and inventing new solutions, knowing more about resources, networks, and projects both for themselves and their clients. They have had to leave their accustomed 'compartments' and work with teachers, counsellors and trainers from the employment agency, entrepreneurs and chambers of commerce, and retired people. Even if all this does not create many jobs, the spin-off is that the relationships created have been rich with potential and energy that can continue to be mobilised. The participation of users in these networks and their management from below mean that new or regenerated networks at grassroots levels create new routes to social *insertion*.

The French association of social workers, *L'Association Nationale des Assistants de Service Social*, ANAS, organised a conference in 1989 on *Assistants Sociaux et RMI*. Denise Jubineau stressed the benefits of the new social action which is now

> becoming a complex field of activity . . . It is the raison d'être of important administrative services at all levels: national, regional, *départemental* communal. It is the domain of employment of numerous and varied professionals. It is giving place to new experiments, to cross-cutting actions where the social is from now on linked to branches formerly distant: the economy, urbanism . . . It is the preoccupation of numerous associations . . . and . . . competent volunteers . . .
>
> The Law of December 1988 on the RMI . . . gave social action a new form: a contractual engagement for the insertion of those

démunis [who are deprived]. Thus, this category of the population will no longer be 'the object of social action' but each
beneficiary (*allocataire*) will have to be considered as a subject
helped in his own way . . . [producing] a profound change in
social action which constitutes a clear advance of democracy.
(Jubineau, 1990, pp. 5–8)

She went on to argue that public organisations would need
to cede some of their power: 'there will be a loss of zones of
power'; there would be less distance between agencies as
they worked together under the scrutiny of the local commis-
sions. Old specialisms could break down and new ones
emerge. One of the most positive aspects of the project is
that social work has a chance to find new ways of working;
there is the opportunity for the practice of the *assistants
sociaux* to become less individualised and for practice to be
renewed, using 'the simple resources of neighbourliness
(*voisinage*) which can be rich in efficacy'.

However, she went on to raise some questions about the
way that social work is being used in this grand project.
There is a threat to the profession's autonomy and a danger
of serving the national and/or local administrations rather
than the 'client', especially as local politicians have become
more determined, powerful and competent since decentralisation. Social work is thus back to its age-old dilemma of to
whom it is accountable: whether the 'client' is the community at large (whatever that may be) or the individual who
requests help. The positives of RMI are that it reorientates
social work to the dynamic between individuals and their
environment, to the material aspects of poverty and to social
work's part in the process of exclusion, and it forces social
work to consider the form relationships with users should
take, especially as it asserts the strengths rather than
pathologies of individuals and communities. A dilemma of
social work, then, is how to participate in this area of work,
and a danger is that if social work raises too many difficulties
a new specialist RMI service will emerge, marginalising social
work. The dilemma is pressing, for the RMI has dramatically
increased the workload and visibility of social workers.

Questions are beginning to emerge. One view is that there
is nothing new in what RMI asks of social workers; that, on

the contrary, it perhaps legitimises the way social workers have always worked and the values they hold. At the same conference Annick Wambst, like Jubineau an *assistante de service sociale*, argued that social workers work daily for *insertion*: 'Perhaps we haven't known well enough how to explain our work. Or perhaps if we are optimists, we have, on the contrary, succeeded in explaining our values. Perhaps the RMI will bring a more official recognition of the knowledge of *assistants sociaux*' (Wambst, 1990, pp. 9–10). She argued that social work is based on respecting the users, helping them to analyse their needs and to develop their capacities and those of their milieux to solve their problems. Social workers have always spent their time communicating with other agencies (such as schools and workplaces), and groups (such as the family or neighbourhood), collecting information, stressing and publicising the needs of marginalised groups and individuals. Social workers are generalists, not concerned with particular problems or age groups, but understanding problems 'in their globality'. At the discussion at the conference, it was agreed that *insertion* carries an ethical dimension: 'the social worker cannot insert a person, it is fundamentally he/she who inserts himself in society' (Cassegrain, 1990, p. 16).

This raises questions as to the notion of contract, which of course is already familiar to *assistants sociaux*:

> It consists of an identification . . . of the questions to be resolved and of a sharing of the tasks between the user and *assistant social* . . . The contract is negotiated between user and professional, it is a real moral engagement between two parties who agree to follow an action. Paulo Freire speaks of the pedagogy of the relation: it is for the professional to give the user a desire to know more, to take on himself in a positive way the means available, to progress in his '*insertion*'. (Wambst, 1990, pp. 9–10)

Marie-Thérèse Paillusson, President of ANAS, reiterated the ambiguities over the contract: 'In our professional vocabulary we understand this to mean something educational, therapeutic, setting plans and objectives. But the RMI contract evokes the contract of work, insurance' (Paillusson, 1990, p. 12).

There is a danger of the contract stopping at statements about training or work. How should the broader elements, the factors that would make *insertion* a positive reality, be expressed? There is a danger that only the concrete factors like courses and tasks will be identified. Then there is the question of whether the contract is a paper relating merely to the institution or to the people involved. What about the obligations of the other partners: are they clear? What sanctions are there against the CLI if it does not fulfil its obligations? Is a contract possible between partners of such different positions (one isolated, one in an organisation)?

French social workers are concerned about the ambiguities which RMI raises for the profession: what about those who do not want to be integrated, who are happy with a life on the margins or who do not wish to change this? What about those who manage better in the informal economy than they would if they 'went straight'? Paradoxically RMI might stigmatise in new ways, by denigrating the choice to remain on the margins (Merlo, 1990). Is there a naivety about the possibility of integration for those who are psychologically vulnerable and may need to remain dependent upon formal sources of care? So French social workers are concerned that the emphasis on employment (albeit in its widest sense) as the route to social integration raises ethical questions about people's choices as to their way of life. For social workers there is a danger that the new focus on results may diminish their focus on and acceptance of the person.

Leonard (1990) has noted that the growth in social work's mandates (child care and protection especially) since 1945 and the impact of decentralisation have meant a progression from a psycho-social credo to something much more concerned with management and cost-effectiveness: 'Closer to the elected (local) politicians, it became more controlled . . . social work was put into a financial framework . . . and forced to reorganise itself, to structure itself and to respond to these objectives: efficacity, profitability, productivity' (Leonard, 1990, p. 36). Social workers (ideally) used to listen to the client, taking what time seemed necessary, making an informal, reciprocal agreement as to the task. Now the client is summoned, has to sign a contract and the work is formalised, with the social worker also under an obligation to achieve a result. The time is limited, and reviews are expected after six months. The social worker is becoming a kind of juridico-administrator more oriented to the economic than the psycho-social; social service has become subordinate to the local politicians and administration, to legal demands, and is in danger of losing sight of the principle of client-centred practice. A danger for users is that social control is becoming personalised, direct, public. Indeed large-scale, collaborative schemes like RMI may increase surveillance, and raise issues of confidentiality.

So some argue that RMI has repositioned social work and that it should take care in being so seduced lest it becomes dulled, blunted and suffocated. Social work should keep its distance, for while RMI opens the doors of legitimacy to social work, it perhaps does so at a cost to social work's autonomy and special concern with the person. As Cocozza (1989) put it in her review of social work training in the EC, the growing concern with *savoir faire* (the expanding field of tasks and projects in which social workers are engaged, the emphasis on competencies) should not be at the expense of *savoir être* (the development of the person). The challenge for French social workers is to keep this *savoir être* in the mainstream, and what follows is a project which aims to do that; it connects the socio-cultural work of *animation* with that of the *assistants sociaux*, illustrating how the contemporary French scene is of a mixing, merging and mutual enrichment of branches of social work.

Le Réseau d'Échanges de Savoirs

While social work has been drawn into the management of unemployment, it is also seizing the chance to put its own imagination into these initiatives. An example of such work is provided by the *Centre Socio-Culturel* in Lisieux, and in particular from its *Réseau d'Échanges de Savoirs* (Network of Knowledge Exchanges). This centre, managed by the *Caisse d'Allocations Familiales*, CAF, is designed to play a primary role in the development of the community and in the amelioration of its image. CAF is the main provider of family and child benefits in France; it is a semi-public body working within government policies and is managed by a national council, composed of various elected representatives of trade unions, associations and other public bodies, designed to give the *allocataires* some power in CAF policies and provision. The state decentralisation prompted CAF's own decentralisation to *département* level in 1983. This means that the kind of services provided varies between areas, according to local agreements as to partnerships and emphasis, but within national minima.

The Centre has a broad field of intervention and it includes its team of social workers and that from the local *secteur* in the *Réseau d'Échanges de Savoirs,* 'which aims for the revalorisation of a public who are particularly damaged (*fragilisê*) by the economic crisis' (CAF de Calvados, 1988). Lisieux has high unemployment (16 per cent in 1989), with recent factory closures and no sign of new industries; this is the key problem. The Centre was established in the *socio-culturel-loisirs* tradition and is managed by an *animateur.* It has, given the rising levels of unemployment, found itself filling gaps in state provision, creating and supporting clubs in order to prevent further or future marginalisation of the local people. The Lisieux team argued that their traditional approach was no longer appropriate in the face of serious social and economic need. They have responded to these needs in a new way (for instance, by tackling adult illiteracy, which only appeared as a problem when people started looking for new work and retraining). The social work team in the Centre is also managed by an *animateur.* The Centre is moving towards increasing partnership with local groups and other organisations: the monthly *Circonscription Sociale* meetings are the means by which the team keep in regular touch with all other local social workers and relevant agencies, whether statutory or independent. The *responsable de circonscription* has an important role in coordinating and developing services: for instance, in monitoring the implementation of the RMI.

The *Réseau d'Échanges de Savoirs* was developed by the *animateur,* who is involved in a national association of such networks. The main principle – like that of some Church-based community projects in the UK – is that the social and moral gap between giver and receiver should be narrowed; everyone should be seen as someone with something to give, and none should only give or only receive. The social workers in the team and in the *secteur* also participate, offering guitar lessons, say, or knitting. A primary aim of the project is to encourage social workers to work in new ways, to modify the images they held of 'clients', to instil some reciprocity into 'client'–professional relationships, and for the Centre to reach and involve 'clients' in a new manner (Arrouet, 1988). The Centre's Report notes that, 'With the establishment of the *Revenue Minimum d'Insertion*, demands for financial help connected to precariousness of situations ought to diminish and allow the social service to favour the autonomy, the valorisation and the social recognition of users' (CAF de Calvados, 1988, p. 5).

The *Réseau* has involved many people (146 in January 1988): in the foyer of the Centre is a noticeboard with large numbers of offers of, and calls for, *savoirs*, such as African cookery, dance, maths, do-it-yourself, budgeting, relaxation, writing, childhood, gardening, foreign languages, general knowledge. The other aims are the amelioration of daily life and a valorisation and development of the person and of the self, by focusing on the positive rather than negative in people. It is open to all, but the hope is that those 'damaged' by a succession of failures will participate, and thus become actors of their destinies.

The project aims to give former 'clients' an awareness of their social usefulness and the possibility, by creating new networks, of asserting their independence. Around 75 per cent of the adults involved in the *Réseau* were known to or referred by the social workers (they were 'clients'). Some knowledge is fairly practical – computing and maths – and designed to get people to try out things they might not otherwise have tried. Retraining and adult professional education are not always easy to find, and in any case some of the people concerned are not yet confident or articulate enough to go straight on to a course. Thus the project is one step back from the RMI (a pre-training stage). However, it also demonstrates the more 'social' aspects of *insertion*, focusing less on formal employment and training, and more on finding what may be suitable or accessible to the more *fragilisés* in the population; this is perhaps a realistic aim because of high unemployment on the one hand, and because of the lack of social skills and literacy in individuals on the other. Of the unemployed of Lisieux 94 per cent have no qualifications. The *Réseau*, however, can help people gain the confidence to go on to formal education or training, or can create work and educational experiences of an informal kind which nevertheless satisfy the RMI requirements.

Two other projects at the Lisieux centre illustrate the new stress on *insertion*. The first linked retired with unemployed people who generally are too ill-educated to find employment or a training course. The retired volunteers, who were generally drawn from an industrial background and had in some cases experienced unemployment themselves, gave courses in French and maths. This project has been extremely successful, both in terms of demand from unemployed people, and their subsequent success in finding some kind of employment or training. The project, named *Le Groupe Retraite-Solidarité* won a prize in 1988 from a pension fund (CRI) for its innovative formula, based on the solidarity of retired persons with those seeking work. However, while there is another wing to this project concerning retired persons and school pupils at risk of failure, the Centre social workers are cautious: 'it is important to maintain the limits of this opération: the help brought by the volunteers cannot be considered as the solution to the deficiencies of the education system aggravated by the economic difficulties of a region' (CAF report, Lisieux 1988, p. 19).

The other project is *Le Programme Local d'Insertion pour Femmes*: 'This action is part of the battery of measures proposed by the Government to fight unemployment. It is essentially concerned with women of more than 40 with insufficient resources. It consists of part work (20 hours per week) and part training, of 6 hours per week over six months.' While the majority of participants in the *Réseau* are women, this project is one with a stronger focus on them as such. Revalorisation of the 'students', through the recovery of confidence in their capacity and an awareness of their knowledge, is the aim. The following section, in looking at social action and child care, will further discuss issues concerning women users.

Social action and child care: CAF's *Centres Sociaux*

CAF's experience of the 'crisis' of the welfare state during the 1970s and 1980s was of rising demands for benefits and growing numbers of 'new poor'; hence it has an economic as well as political interest in preventive action. It has always had a social work wing, providing social aid to its families (including, for instance, holiday centres and children's homes as well as casework for families in difficulty), but now its social work has undergone a major re-think. Allying itself firmly with government thinking on the importance of maintaining social solidarity and *insertion* by developing neighbourhoods and reaching *les précaires* (literally those in precarious social positions), it announced in 1987 that social action would henceforth be part of its policies of supporting the family, and that social work would be one of the means of developing this mission (CNAF, 1987–8). CAF's social workers are in the main *assistants de service sociaux* (family social workers) and *conseillèurs en économic sociale et familiale* (family advisers); also, in much smaller numbers, *puéricultrices* (health visitors) and *animateurs*. The family benefits and social action are provided in separate wings of CAF so that social workers are not directly involved in income maintenance work; rather, the social action wing is a complement to the benefits system, together adding up to a policy of supporting the family through universal (and some targeted) provision.

CAF's priorities are, in addition to the general aim of supporting the family whatever its form, to improve services for 0–6-year-olds, to reach isolated mothers, and to work with young people at risk of unemployment, these latter two categories being subsumed under the aim of *l'insertion des plus fragiles*. Its family benefits are generous, reflecting natalist family policy. The French view is that children are future citizens of the state; the paternalistic state therefore assumes responsibility for them rather than assuming they are private indulgences of parents (Baker, 1986). The family as a basic unit of solidarity is supported, and while this means a certain conservatism over gender roles, the French mother is assumed to need help in her domestic tasks; leisure and holidays are seen as promoting her healthy functioning. Children, too, are thought to need services in their own right, so there is extensive after-school and holiday provision, and a system of holiday vouchers for both parents and children.

The new social action is placed in *centres sociaux*, which complement the *centres communal d'action sociale*, and other municipal services such as the *maisons des jeunes* and *crèches*. They are located in areas where they provide family services and promote local social development. The centres in Normandy are impressively modern, well designed and equipped, with plenty of space for their teams and users. They all have *halte garderies*; nurseries for children who may be left for up to 20 hours per week, on demand, at a token fee. These complement the *crèches* which are provided by CAF and/or the municipality for children of working mothers. The centres are, for the most part, on large modern estates with a mix of housing and a clientele from a range of backgrounds and ethnic groups. The workers in all the centres, however, are aware of growing problems of poverty, especially among single parents and the young unemployed, and of other problems such as the isolation of second-generation ethnic minority children, or the emotional poverty of some children's lives. While emphasising reaching these groups and compensating for disadvantages, there was a prevalent view that the social work task was to promote harmonious relationships among social groups, and thus to work with a range of groups, not just the most deprived. There is a commitment to making the centre a common space for local users, to stimulating and animating a variety of groups and interests, and thus altering the ecology of the neighbourhood.

Social work and social action address different levels of problems in the same centres. There are, for instance, compensatory education sessions for children whose lives are seriously deprived by being often left alone in flats while parents work in the informal economy. Families under court-ordered supervision (*tutelle*) use these centres to meet specialist social workers (*délégués*). There are *assistantes sociales* with caseloads including child protection work overseen by the Children's Judge, and there is generally available parent-advice work carried out by *conseillèurs d'économie sociale et familiale*. There is a *puéricultrice* who carries out the statutory preventive infant and maternal welfare services (*Protection Maternelle et Infantile* or PMI), and there may be sessions with the infant welfare doctor, with psychologists or with other remedial therapists. Some have *animateurs*. Within this framework there is some variation: for instance, in the amount of attention given to cultural activities (or *animation*), and in the representation of other departments (such as housing or mental health) and of the benefits side of CAF.

The attitude of CAF and its social workers is that groups 'at risk' should be helped to discover and to express their citizenship by participating in services and institutions designed for the whole community or area, rather than receiving targeted services. This can require some change on the part of 'normal' people (those not identified as clients or deviants), whose attitudes are crucial to the inclusion of the poor and vulnerable. It also requires a change from professionals, increasingly working alongside and animating the strengths of communities rather than monitoring and controlling their weaknesses. Thus social workers emphasise the work of revalorisation, and their clubs and activities are designed to provide settings and opportunities for participation and for the mixing of social groups.

Participation, the essence of social action, is not easy to develop: *animateurs* are used to working with stable working-class communities; the Centres have a social mix, and the *défavorisés* (underprivileged) do not participate in the same way as 'normal' users. There can be conflict between different groups, but it is this segregation which CAF workers are trying to change (for instance, through the *Réseau d'Échanges des Savoirs*). The *crèches* and *halte garderies* are beginning to think of more involvement and participation of parents, but until now these have been child-centred, providing compensatory experiences for the child but not acting on their familial or social environment. And finally, the pressing tasks of contemporary social work – child protection and RMI – can push social action down the list of priorities. However, it did appear from the author's fieldwork that French social workers were far more able than English social workers (in area teams or in family centres) to keep open the generalist aspects of their work, partly because of good *crèche* and *halte garderie* provision.

A recent piece of research by CAF social workers in Normany found that many children did not go away on holiday in July and August, so a programme of activities was established for those who remained at home. This project – *Action Été Vacances* – has developed from national crime prevention initiatives. The 1984–8 National Plan called for a special emphasis on youth, with the establishment of youth and community centres and a massive programme of summer activities known as *Action Étés Jeunes* (M. King, 1988). These schemes are funded by the government via the municipalities, and all young people can claim a holiday. Cities have established Delinquency Prevention Councils – partnerships of social, youth, sport and police organisations and politicians – to work out local strategies. The CAF project, run in partnership with the independent *Loisirs Quotidien des Jeunes*, makes sure that children get financial help for *Colonies de vacances* or other holiday centres, or that they are involved in activities in their own community. Children are socially mixed in order to avoid stigmatisation or a concentration of problems or of particular groups (for instance, children of North African origin). The notion of entitlement to a holiday is an old one in France, and recent delinquency prevention schemes have expanded already extensive holiday activity schemes.

RMI has meant there has been new thinking on how people should be integrated. Social workers face the less easy cases for integration – the deteriorated, alcoholic, or people with mental health problems – who are unlikely to find training courses. They try to find ideas for work that meet the criteria for *insertion*, such as cleaning up entrances to flats and the surrounding area, or helping a neighbour, or doing motor mechanics. Statutory work – RMI and child protection – must be carried out by the social workers in addition to the overall social action brief. One way in which social workers keep a sense of direction is via meetings of the *circonscription sociale*.

Responsable de circonscription sociale, Hérouville St Clair

It is appropriate here to give an indication as to how the *responsable de circonscription sociale* can influence and coordinate social intervention across a district (*circonscription*). This is a post which connects social work across different agencies and various branches of social work, as well as drawing in other agencies such as the police, schools or local tradesmen. The *responsables* in the Caen and Hérouville area were doing a considerable amount of work with *assistants sociaux*, who tend to be anxious and resistant about being pushed into collective action rather than working with individuals. They are seen as needing education in politics and organisations, in *action collectif*, and in changing their methods and mentality lest the *animateurs* and *conseilleurs en ESF* move into their field, (these two branches of social work being more accustomed to, and trained in, working with groups). RMI is helping with raising awareness of collective work aimed at *insertion*. The *responsable* helps social workers think out their strategies and approaches in the new methods and projects, and to deal with the pressures of the statutory work. The *responsable* may do research into the needs of the district or the incidence of problems in order to make more effective use of services and resources.

In Hérouville there is a lot going on in the field of *animation*, especially in delinquency prevention projects such as motor workshops. There are many youth problems: drugs, lack of leisure facilities, nothing to do in the evenings. Drunkenness is a problem so a non-alcohol café is being started. Projects encouraged by the *circonscription* include:

1. an alcohol prevention scheme;
2. a parents' pre-school preparation group;
3. HABITAT (renovation scheme) by the city involving users and social workers:
4. *Réseau d'Échanges de Savoirs*;

5. *Ateliers d'aide langage* (language workshops: all ethnic groups, but especially 'immigrants', 12 per cent of the local population);
6. *Une mutuelle*, which means creating a fund for those who do not use health, dental, and optical services because social security does not reimburse the total sum (that is, increasing use of health services);
7. *Réseau de prévention*: an informal network of people with knowledge of alcoholism, contraception, etc. run by users and locals after being established by professionals.

These schemes have been established on a huge modern estate, a new city, now showing familiar social problems of isolation and depression among women, especially single parents and elderly women. There is considerable poverty and unemployment, and the introduction of RMI has galvanised local responses. There are 'immigrants' and foreigners without professional/educational/skills qualifications, and adult illiteracy. The youth problems have received considerable attention because of the concerted national and local efforts described earlier in the chapter in integrating young people and involving them in socio-cultural pursuits.

Discussion: social work and citizenship

This chapter has been concerned with the way in which the clientele of social agencies has been reconceptualised. The discourses on *insertion* and *exclusion* are part and parcel of the restructuring of the welfare state, and the reshaping of social work's role within it. Especially in the community care field, social work's function is the transformation of relationships with 'clients' so that as users they create (produce) new means of meeting social and personal needs. The issue is whether these new means are merely cost-cutting, management-down exercises, or whether they can work to the benefit of users. We consider that the French experience while containing both these elements, is based on extensive social practices much more favourably balanced *vis-à-vis* users (and the community as a whole) than is the case in the more stringent economic and ideological climate in the UK.

The Socialist decentralisation claimed to represent a spread of democracy; at local levels there is still so much change and variation that it is not possible to give a definitive picture of the extent to which this is so. The left came to power in 1981, committed to the modernisation and transformation of society and especially of the economy. Much of its politics had rested on the slogan of *autogestion* (self-management), with roots in '68ers' and a romantic grassroots impulse. But the *Partie Socialiste* (PS) which left power in 1986 had moved into the politics of *rigueur*, and a certain affinity with the new right's criticisms of the welfare state for inefficiency and work disincentives (Ross, 1987). Now the welfare state, at first relatively well endowed by the PS, was portrayed as expensive and as having social costs. The new social action and the decentralisation initiative derive their logic from the drive to modernise the economy and thus the nation.

Decentralisation has not introduced new forms of democracy as hoped for by the *autogestionaires*. While the *préfets* have lost much of their power (formerly they were the state's representative at local level), now new local political entrepreneurs, *élus* (elected, councillors at various levels) and *éminences grises* have merged (Mény, 1987). Decentralisation is viewed by some as having merely shifted burdens from central to local government, with the centre keeping considerable power through financial grants, technical specifications, and its power to set in motion large-scale programmes. Some have seen it as a spread and dispersal of state power, accompanied by a new layer of powerful local politicians (Garrish, 1986).

These politicians influence (and derive power from) local social action and social prevention projects via membership of, for instance, the crime prevention committees, or the *CLIs*. This means that social workers are not only working under greater public scrutiny than previously, but that they are faced with the issue of in whose interests they should work, and of whether the elected politicians (of right or left) can be said to represent the poor. No wonder, then, that French social workers are concerned that they may be (insidiously) expanding their social control of the poor. The dilemma is acute, for the future of social work – for instance, in the expansion of training – may depend on participation in state social policies. As we have shown in this chapter, social workers are discussing their attitude to people who may not want to be integrated. Of those who do, how much power do the users really have in shaping the project of *insertion*, and how much influence do social workers have in broadening ideas as to what constitutes suitable integrative activities? We have shown that in their valorisation of their traditional clientele social workers have gone a good way towards raising public awareness of the existence of the underclass, yet this work of valorisation is now being turned back on to social workers with perhaps an unrealistic challenge: social work must guard against becoming a substitute for adequate industrial investment and the improvement of the education system.

There are also dangers of social work becoming involved in discriminatory employment programmes. Young women (and especially those from ethnic minorities) are at risk of unemployment or precarious employment. However, because young women so often solve their problems of employment by falling into the traditional role of motherhood they are perceived as less of a public threat than young men and, to the extent that they are a threat, they are 'supported' by family services rather than training (Lagrée and Lew Fai, 1987). The Socialists' policies to promote women's rights in the fields of employment and training in the early 1980s were downplayed from 1984 onwards in favour of family policy, with natalist language and traditional gender roles (Reynolds, 1988).

Conclusion

Social work in France is much absorbed in issues to do with user-involvement, parallelling debates in the UK on participation. How can social workers promote bottom-up forms of participation? While the drift of policy may be towards top-down forms of user involvement, social workers are well

positioned to influence schemes to promote as much genuine user involvement as possible (see Beresford and Croft,
1990, for examples).

What seems to us to be useful in the French approach is
the strong sense of 'society' and of solidarity. The British new
right has a concept of citizenship that is an individualist,
private form of self-reliance (Lister, 1990). By contrast, like
much of European Socialism, Catholicism and paternalistic
conservatism, the French philosophy emphasises participation as an integral part of citizenship, essential to the health
of society as a whole. Citizens, in this view, need to be given
the means to exercise their social rights of citizenship, and
these means include generally available services such as education, housing and cultural activities. Social action is an
attempt imaginatively to reinforce participation through formal means (such as employment and training), and informal
and social means (such as involvement in networks of neighbourliness and community, of child care and of culture).
Certainly in the latter the French approach is notably different from the British: social workers are reformulating their
relationships with users by expanding the range of social
groups with whom they work.

Finally, then, it seems that French social workers are showing that social work needs to avoid its own marginalisation if
it is to promote integration and to shape debates about ways
and means. While finding that public scrutiny raises issues
for autonomy and accountability, social work is nevertheless
poised to influence social policies and to negotiate its position within them at both national and local levels. We shall
continue with these themes by moving now to look at some
social work initiatives in Germany, using them to expand our
discussion of participation and social rights.

6

Participation: A European Ideal and a Social Work Activity

Introduction

The EC is concerned not only with economic but also social issues, and in particular the desire to promote social harmony and cooperation. In order to make these concerns tangible and influential, the EC has created structures and initiatives which have begun to exemplify a commitment to a pluralist and participatory form of representation. This democratic vision of participation, integration and solidarity is held by both the EC and the Council of Europe. This ideal is obviously not limited to Western Europe, but is one of the most important political and philosophical forces of the later part of the twentieth century. It has fuelled the explosion of democratic and participatory rhetoric by the governments, as well as the people, of much of the world. The 'new order' has been demonstrated in the broader political movements of the right as well as the left, and a new language of participation, integration and involvement has been coined.

Participation means many things, and in Chapter 1 we looked at some of the programmes of the EC and the ways in which they promoted economic, social and political integration and unity. Amongst the forms of participation they promoted were:

1. individual and national participation in the representative institutions of Europe;

2. Community participation in economic and social programmes of regeneration;
3. participation by groups of people who have been marginalised and disadvantaged;
4. individual participation through the systems of legal review and redress, and through the promotion of social rights.

In this chapter we shall examine the ways in which this European ideal has underwritten and reinforced social work's commitments to participation.

The ideal of participation for the citizen and the worker has been reinforced through the development of the charter of social rights for workers, the 'Social Charter' of 1990 (Commission of the EC 1990b). Jacques Delors' emphasis on social partners has been one way of demonstrating this commitment to participation. Another has been through the subsequent charters for particular groups, such as elderly people and children. This creation of a series of rights, including the right to participate, has also become a more important aspect of social work in many European countries.

For British social work the idea of rights is a very important consequence of the mood and philosophy of the European ideal. Within this there is a tension (discussion in Chapter 1) between, on the one hand, the idea of individual freedom from regulation and, on the other, the vision of creating cooperation. It is also about enhancing the collective power of the Community over that of any individual member state. This conflict expresses itself as one between protection and regulation, a tension well understood in social work. The way it has been expressed through the development of charters of rights, and the use of formal contracts to ensure quality and accountability, is not directly dependent upon any specific European initiative; rather it is a reflection of a more pervasive philosophical and organisational change in the delivery of social work.

Charters of rights have gained rapid headway in many service economies and sectors, not only those of social care. At the end of the 1980s they were seen as part of a radical left-wing strategy, tackling the power of the state on behalf of certain oppressed groups. By the 1990s they have become part of the everyday consumerist language of any public or private service. Each political party issued its own Charter of Rights and, under John Major, the British Conservative Party introduced a Citizen's Charter in 1991. This codifies many of the steps towards participation and accountability that had already been underway within the health, education, social and other public services. It does this in a language which reflects and complements some of the language of the Social Charter in a way that would have been unlikely a little while earlier.

This sea change in the language and the promotion of this overarching view of participation has begun to affect the formulation of social work issues throughout Europe and in the member states. We shall later consider how participation has emerged as a social work issue in what was West Germany and in Britain.

Participation and social work: EC projects for citizenship

The idea of participation, it is argued here, has created a context within which integration and involvement, partnership and accountability have become bywords. Social work operates within the tension of protection and regulation. Does the way in which the EC defines social need help or hinder the task of social workers in enabling disadvantaged and marginalised people to exercise their rights to participation? We shall consider whether the EC is 'social-work friendly': whether it encourages social workers to look at it as a source of information or action on social issues and what steps have been taken to acknowledge the role of social work in promoting participation.

The European context has been important to social workers in different member states in various ways. Although the Community is not concerned directly with social work activities, it has produced a number of programmes (discussed in Chapter 1) with very similar interests to those of social work.

Social workers have been most involved with the second and third categories of programmes outlined above, those that are concerned with social and economic regeneration. They have been interested in using the EC programmes of integration to promote the participation of disadvantaged communities and groups. In addition social workers have been concerned with the fourth category of participation, that which is interested in the individual's participation in systems of legal review, and also in individual rights. In particular there has been a growing involvement with the legislative processes which have promoted greater equality and access to social assistance, and in the individual judgements of the Court of Human Rights and the European Court of Justice in relation to specific social work cases (see Hillestad Thune, 1987).

Participation is both a locally negotiated concept, and one that has been promoted by the programmes of the EC. The particular histories, constitution and indeed welfare systems of the member countries have produced many ideas about what it is to participate. Services have been established, organised and managed in many ways. This has influenced the relationship that the users and providers of services have, and the expectations they have of each other.

Even the term participation does not have one definition. In the same way as the words 'federal' and 'integrated' have no agreed meaning for the governments of Britain and the mainland European countries, these terms have a different philosophical as well as political implication. It may be that the term participation is not as useful as, say, integration, insertion or solidarity (for example, see Chapter 5 on the French programmes of social action), and that rights have another value in a country with a constitution that proclaims a right to social help, as in Germany. Consequently, within these social services organisations participation will reflect many social welfare paradigms not only in each member state, but also in the institutions of Europe themselves.

The first category of participation, that of individual and national participation in the representative institutions of Europe, has perhaps least affected social work, but there are some examples of the way in which this has been important. One way is through the promotion of consumer charters. Other important ways have been through action research and lobbying organisations and bodies, such as those either funded by the EC or focusing their activities on the objectives of the EC. In order to promote participation in the institutions and programmes of Europe, the Commission has funded a number of projects to enable people from disadvantaged groups and communities to act as its advisers. In the field of consumer affairs, for example, a three-year action programme was launched by the EC in March 1989, which incorporated legislative changes and the issuing of Guidance. It also created a Consultative Council and outreach work to promote the development of consumer representation in the peripheral regions. This model is not unusual within the broad spectrum of social affairs, and it is becoming more common within those social-work related activities of services for elderly and disabled people and other marginal groups.

The work of DG5, EC's Directorate-General for Social Affairs, has been very influential in creating ways of hearing the views of people with disabilities, people disadvantaged by failings in the systems of education and training, women's groups, and so on. Furthermore, EC-supported bodies such as CREW (the Centre for Research on European Women) and the Women's Lobby have been active in researching and campaigning on social-work related issues such as pensions, education, abortion, poverty and care for elderly people. The IRIS network (European Network of Training Schemes for Women), which is managed and coordinated by CREW, is an example of the type of initiative of the European Commission that exists not only to research into women's affairs but also to network between projects in the member states. It has created a forum in which women from different areas can put forward model initiatives, so that the cumulative knowledge can be used to influence European and national policy-making.

Other organisations, such as IULA (the International Union of Local Authorities), have focused on the activities of the Commission to promote social affairs issues and legislation. This has included the protection of children and adolescents, social protection and care for people with mental illnesses, and the care of elderly people. IULA has been influential in assessing the problems that local authorities have experienced, or may experience, with EC law. Amongst their particular concerns they have identified thirteen major areas. Nearly half are of direct concern to social workers: the protection of children and adolescents; the needs of disabled people; the improvement of living and working conditions; the social care of the elderly people; social protection; and social housing. Their intention is to promote a dialogue between European local authorities, the users of their services and the European Commission on social affairs.

Participation in decision-making has been seen as an important goal of the EC. On the whole this has been viewed in relation to those decisions that affect communities and interest groups, not those that affect individual citizens. The idea of the citizen has, however, become important. People power seemed to be on the agenda of the new Europe, and this was reflected in the debates and activities of the EC in the late 1980s. This was reinforced by a number of Resolutions of the Council of Europe which promoted the idea of participation, and the importance of citizen involvement in local government. One such was a Resolution accepted by the Standing Conference of Local and Regional Authorities in Europe, in March 1989. Resolution 208, on self-help and community development in towns, called for an expansion of support for community development programmes by local authorities and others, and for a promotion of the principles and practice of community development throughout the member states. Its purpose was to enable local communities to gain the skills and confidence to engage in local decision-making about resources, and to act 'as a mechanism for the stimulation of local solidarity, the local economy and a sense of citizenship' (Council of Europe, March 1989).

The European Commission has established a limited number of programmes which put these ideas into effect, such as the Leemar programme. This was set up to look at European regions in decline and in transition, and designed to bring community organisations across Europe together to share experience.

John Benington, an Assessor of the Third Poverty Programme, has described this as a 'programme which didn't produce very much money but which did, at least, bring those regions and many of their community organisations together; a mechanism for bringing community organisations in local authorities from Europe together to share experience' (in McConnell, 1990).

The ERGO Programme, created specifically for the long-term unemployed, has also brought little money, but it has supported groups to establish unemployment resource centres where people meet together, to network and to build exchanges of experience, and exchange feelings of solidarity (McConnell, 1990).

Organisations have been established to foster these ideas. These include the European Citizen's Action Service (ECAS). Its director, Tony Venables, described its function as being to promote the idea of a citizen's Europe, in order to involve people in European policies and legislation through their membership of organisations that protect their rights, social welfare, health, environment, etc. (McConnell, 1990). It grew out of the European consumer movement to help voluntary and community organisations find their way through the European maze.

The view of this organisation and of many others is that a citizen's Europe is more about the Europe of associations and organisations than about individuals. Venables has said that in his view the individual has little power within the fragmented departments of the Commission: 'I think that it is far too optimistic, as there is no mechanism whereby individuals in 12 countries can really bring weight to bear on the EC' (McConnell, 1990). He sees the role of ECAS as being about promoting collective weight rather than individual petition.

Other undertakings have also been instituted to promote participation and integration in the European-wide community. They have been aimed at the priority groups of disadvantaged and marginalised people and communities, such as young people from minority ethnic groups, disabled people and women. Projects involving exchanges and work experience in other countries have been developed, such as one which was part-funded by European business interests and partly by DG5 to set up an Innovatory Training Unit. The purpose of this was to set up a training and education unit for people from minority ethnic groups and migrant peoples in the UK, the Netherlands and Belgium. It was based in national institutes for social work and community development in these countries. It drew on action research in nine European countries, arranged exchanges of 'trainees', held study seminars in six countries (Belgium, West Germany, Luxembourg, the Netherlands, France and the UK), and enabled the participants, all from minority and marginalised groups, to make a submission to DG5 and to the Commission on its social and economic development programmes for minority groups (Thomas, van Rees and Swinnen, 1989).

These types of initiative have reflected the concerns of social workers across Europe, and have often been established by social and community workers simultaneously 'learning the system' and establishing projects. An argument often made against these programmes is that they affect so few people, and are what Townsend (1990), for one, has described as 'puny' because there is so little budgetary investment. This is certainly true, although some contain major research, pilot and action programmes, ensuring that their significance far outweighs their apparent size. In Chapter 1, the best known of the initiatives – the poverty programme – was discussed. This programme has been vital in enabling local people at a regional level to have their voices heard in the development of the Commission's economic and social policies.

Less well known (but extremely interesting) work has come out of the research and development projects of the European Foundation for the Improvement of Living and Working Conditions (EFILWC). It is a relatively small organisation, but its influence has become considerable in affecting the social policy of the Commission, and indeed the views of the all-important Council of Ministers. The European Foundation was established by the Council of Ministers in 1975, and receives funding from the European Parliament. One strand of its current programmes of work is called 'Raising the quality and standard of life for all'. The projects include: coping with social and economic change at a neighbourhood level; counselling the long-term unemployed; accommodation and social cohesion (the implications for young people); family care of the older elderly; and consumer-oriented action in public services (EFILWC, 1991).

This programme was set up to address what were felt to be the new forms of exclusion and poverty experienced by people living in the marginal areas of Europe. Others of its programmes could become influential in the debate on the organisation and management of social care in Britain. One, on community care for elderly people, looks at the plurality of provision and the use of volunteers, and another at consumer-orientation in public services. The preliminary studies for the programmes were undertaken in Spain and Portugal, and underline the changing patterns of social care of elderly people. The fieldwork for these began in the autumn of 1990, documenting the problems of family carers, and the contribution to care of public, private and voluntary provision of services. The results of the work are expected to have implications for policies on housing and employment, as well as those concerned with social security and the welfare sectors, and will be incorporated into the Commission's Action Programme for elderly people.

One of the Foundation's projects – counselling long-term unemployed people – is an interesting example of the way in which social work concerns and those of the economic agendas come together. This particular project comes under the theme of 'living conditions', and has as its context the overall objectives of 'raising the standard and quality of life for all: social cohesion and groups at risk'.

Its aims are:

1. to extend and deepen the Foundation's work on means to improve the quality of life for the long-term unemployed and to facilitate their re-integration into social and economic life;
2. to enhance the quality and effectiveness of counselling, information, advice and guidance services for the long-term unemployed;
3. to encourage networking, joint initiatives, exchanges of good practice and ideas at a local level between all the different agencies providing counselling services for the long-term unemployed;

4. to elaborate methods which can be used to stimulate the development of more effective systems at local level, which focus on meeting the needs of those experiencing or facing long-term unemployment.

The work is based on a number of principles, which have particular resonance for social work activities. First, it sees counselling as a 'central activity in an integrated sequence of measures to improve the situation for the long term unemployed', and 'that counselling and the systems which provide it are not effective enough to meet the needs of the long term unemployed'; there are also benefits of involving those responsible for the provision and planning of counselling services in a programme of action research'.

This action research programme is based in six member states, promotes cooperation and the sharing of experiences across these countries and also promotes new initiatives. The users of these counselling services are involved in their development and planning, and it is undertaken in conjunction with the EC's ERGO Programme and CEDEFOP (*Centre européen pour la promotion de la formation professionnelle*, or European centre for professional training).

Although many of the organisations involved will be employers and trade unions, the involvement of more traditional welfare organisations will also form an important element. The intention is that it will 'monitor the policy implication of [its] activities, involve policy makers in the initiatives and ensure the findings are speedily passed to EC policy makers, national governments, and the social partner's organisations'. This sort of project may sound a long way from social work as it is often described in the UK, but it is an example of the sort of initiative that has some effect on bringing together the policy and practice concerns of the EC to create a social response.

The approach has already had some influence in Britain, where the Department of Employment is undertaking a similar pilot project promoting specialist counselling services for long-term unemployed people through a voluntary organisation, FWA (Family Welfare Association).

These sorts of initiative are very much influenced by the second and third categories of European participation: that is, the participation in the economic and social concerns of the community to promote social cohesion and integration. This type of participation is important for social work in its European context. It gives a rationale and a legitimacy for collective action and for social development methodologies and interventions.

Individual rights and the new charters

For many British social workers the essence of social work is the way in which it affects the individual. We have seen how the forms of participation encouraged by the European Commission have largely been about the community or about groups of people. Other aspects of participation and the European vision have also been significant and, as was discussed in earlier chapters, the EC has tried to develop integration through the dual approach of solidarity and subsidiarity. The notion of subsidiarity is important here as it relates to the idea of privacy and freedom from interference. The view of the Commission is that there should be a hierarchy of involvement when there are problems, starting at the level of the family, moving to the local community, and then (only in the last resort) having to involve the state to provide support. This, combined with the idea of privacy and freedom from restriction on individuals, have been guiding principles of the economic and social policies of the EC. Unfortunately, together with the limited powers of the Parliament, this has tended to reinforce the idea that individual concerns and petition will have little effect.

However, many individual European citizens have looked to Europe as a means of setting right injustices and discrimination, and the creation of sets of individual rights. Even where they have only moral, and not formal, jurisdiction the influence of the European Courts has become most significant. The Council of Europe's report on the Proceedings of the Joint Meeting on Human Rights and Social Workers in Strasbourg, 1987, details interesting examples of the ways in which these have begun to influence social work.

The development of the idea of rights at both individual and group level, and the tension between them, is crucial. As an idea it is, of course, not new and each country has its own history and tradition. In particular the British experience has promoted different sets of demands: those of the consumer and those of the oppressed. The language of rights was last fashionable in Britain in the 1960s and 1970s, when social campaigners pressed for welfare and legal rights against the actions of the state. Now the rights that are being described are those of the consumer. Groups and individuals, who would previously have been thought to have rescinded their rights by becoming dependent on the state, are now presumed to have the new rights of customer and citizen.

Recent British social work has brought these two sets of demands more closely together, producing charters of rights and customer contracts for service users. Clients or users are seen as participants who have become partners in the development of social work. They are viewed as citizens who have paid for services either directly or indirectly, and to whom the providers of services should be accountable. Furthermore they are being seen as having rights within social services legislation to disagree and complain, to be given information, to see files, to participate in decision-making, and to receive services of an assured quality. This emphasis on rights is not confined to the world of social welfare: rather it is part of a consumerist trend in many public services (including health, education, housing, and through the privatisation of basic amenities). It is supported by central and local government policies from all political parties. It is a manifestation of the sorts of concern embodied in Charter 88, the Conservative Party's Citizen's Charter (1991) and some of the new cross-party moves to consensus politics and proportional representation.

It has been given an additional air of modernity by being wrapped up in the mantle of new Europeanism, based on constitutions, agreements and responsibilities. Britons, previously proud of their lack of a constitution, have been persuaded to accept new administrative systems, legal frameworks and methods of judicial review. These have created a new basis for systems of rights, participation, social and economic justice, with a European flavour.

This, at least, is what the rhetoric suggests. This European ideal has coloured the language of everything from political advertising to the information given to users of these social services. However, it is worth considering whether rights really are being created, and whether the charters are more than a façade behind which practice continues much as before.

The Social Charter

The European Social Charter contains a variety of rights in relation to work and labour in general, together with rights of protection for special groups such as children and young people, for trade unions, and the right of protection of social institutions such as the family. Chapter 1 details its remit more extensively. The Charter is a dynamic force, and as such has always reflected changing social needs and aspirations. It has never been without controversy, illustrating the ambivalence felt about creating common European social expectations, particularly those regulating the relationship between the individual and the state.

The importance of the Social Charter at present cannot be overestimated as a rallying cry and statement of intent for developing a notion of integrated European social rights. However, there remains some ambivalence about the potential of charters of rights. Although they can list certain broadly agreed demands, in a social work setting these rights will be culturally interpreted and negotiated, and yet they will be expected to affect standards, practices and the outcomes of social work interventions. If the EC were to lay down a charter of social rights, it would be difficult to monitor and enforce such rights without them being locally negotiated. On the other hand, as a statement of basic principles, such Charters have already begun to have an important influence.

The Charter for Elderly People

The European Commission's resolution on *Community Actions for the Elderly* is an example of the type of document that is being described as a charter. This was published by the European Commission in April 1990. It is often assumed that the charters present a delineated series of rights. This is not so; instead, they create a framework and a strategy.

Taking the Social Charter as its starting point, the Charter for Elderly People, for example, produces an analysis of the current situation of elderly people, considers the implications of an ageing population, reviews the position of elderly people as a positive resource, and then proposes a number of measures.

It limits itself, within the principles of subsidiarity, to the position that: 'The Community cannot substitute for measures taken in Member States at the appropriate level . . . the Community should limit its role to encouraging the exchange of information and experience as well as the transfer of knowledge and innovative initiatives on topics of common interest' (para, 48: Communication on the Elderly, Commission of the EC (1990a), 80, 24 April 1990). It then codifies the legal instruments already adopted concerning elderly people, and the various recommendations that the Commission has already made. Finally it sets out a series of activities over a three-year period to promote greater knowledge, exchanges and events, and 'the networking of innovative experiences'.

The resolution incorporated these elements into a proposal with the following objectives:

1. to contribute to the development of preventive strategies to meet the economic and social challenges of an ageing population;
2. to identify innovative approaches to strengthening solidarity between the generations and integration of the elderly population, involving all economic and social agents, in rural as well as urban contexts;
3. to develop and highlight the positive potential of elderly citizens in contributing to the Community.

It also suggested the activities necessary to achieve these objectives. These include the creation of networks for the exchange of experiences and information, the preparation of special projects to promote innovative experiences, the creation of a data bank, and the promotion of a European Year. The year 1993 has been designated the European Year of the Elderly and Solidarity between the Generations.

The Second International Congress of Directors of Residential Homes for the Aged (held in the autumn of 1991) introduced a social charter defining the rights of elderly people, and thus the rights of elderly people living in institutions. Earlier, the journal *Ageing in Europe*, January 1991, used the opportunity to review the progress of such Charters throughout Europe. It is evident that many countries are using the opportunity, initiated by the EC, to create manifestos concerned with promoting the dignity and independence of elderly people.

This Congress of Directors has codified many local initiatives and produced its own composite Charter. The rights it claims are:

> Freedom of choice; freedom not to lose independence; to determine one's own living and housing conditions; to enjoy a variety of relationships; to maintain relationships with families and friends; to financial security; to participate in public life; to religious freedom; to prevent dependence; to be cared for by qualified caretakers; to receive information and to be fully integrated into society. (Ageing in Europe, 1991, Senioren-Charta, 1990)

The strength of a European-wide approach is that it gives support and recognition to a variety of approaches to problems, and suggests strategies that might be transferable to different countries.

Social work, empowerment and participation in Germany and Britain

Within a European context, we have seen the emergence of the idea of rights and, in particular, the right of participation. In this section we shall review some of the practices and policies in two countries to try to understand this more concretely.

Participation has been the subject of considerable debate and discussion in Britain. The work of Ann Richardson (1983) Christine Hallet (1987) and Peter Beresford and Suzy Croft (1986) has done much to develop this debate. Rather than rehearse the different models, it is sufficient to say that participation is not a value-free concept, and that there may be very different motives for encouraging it when welfare is expanding, and when it is under threat. None the less we are of the view that, despite some of the problems, it is important to try to enable the voices of users to be heard in policy-making, resource allocation and the development of practice.

Most European social work practitioners would acknowledge that the recipients of their services and interventions should have certain basic rights. Most users would also think so. However, the very marginalisation and lack of power of many of the users of services or recipients of assistance has meant that the champions of the rights have often come from within the systems themselves.

In Britain these champions have tended to focus on the rights of voluntary and involuntary recipients of services. In other European countries the emphasis has been not so much on the rights of people after they have received the service, but rather on creating a system in which the users have a plurality of choice, and a system which should react responsibly and effectively to their needs.

British social workers speak about wanting to empower users against the weight of the state (that is, the social services department or the benefits system) and to use their social work skills to do so. Those in the former West Germany wish to empower people to choose between different providers of service, and to have their needs properly met within a system of insurance benefits. They tend to concentrate on systems and structures. As the concept of participation is culturally and socially created, so too is the definition of rights. The new Germany may pose different questions about the rights of people to receive services, and for them to be delivered through particular structures.

Discussions held before and after German reunification have emphasised that, although the former West German social system is to be established throughout Germany, it will have to be modified to accommodate Eastern and Western expectations of the state. (Note that most of the research for this chapter was based in what was West Germany but, as this system is also being established in the East, references here to 'Germany' will mean both parts.)

In Britain the rights of social services clients have tended to be promoted by local charters, complaints procedures, access to records, and participative practices such as joint recording. In the wider poverty field and social action campaigns, concern tended to centre around the rights of claimants articulated by the welfare rights movements, collective action, tenants' associations, etc. These activities may have been undertaken by social workers in the British sense, but more likely they will have been undertaken by people who would describe themselves as neighbourhood workers, project workers, and so on.

These same people would in Germany probably describe themselves as either social workers or social pedagogues. The form of participation with which they would be involved would be more likely to centre around the self-help movement, and enabling small groups of people to set up services for themselves or others.

In Germany, representational boards have been established to review the provision of services in a locality. These are for such groups as elderly people, and those with a physical disability. Social workers try to ensure that potential users sit on these committees, seeing empowerment as including involvement in the process of determining service contracts.

It is an oversimplification, but there does seem to be a tendency in Britain to see empowerment as something that social workers become involved in once people have become recipients of services. In Germany the focus of empowerment and participation is not so much on the individual and issues of practice, but rather on the process of community involvement.

Discussions with the Head of Social Policy for elderly people at the *Paritätischer Wohlfahrtsverband* (DPWV), which acts as an umbrella body for many of the non-religious voluntary organisations, emphasised the role of self-help groups and membership of the local boards and committees as the major means of participation for users. The structures and systems, together with the establishment and support of self-help groups, seem to be the ways in which users' voices are most commonly heard.

Self-help groups are, however, generally supported by and employ professional social work staff. An organisation such as the VAMV, *Verband alleinstehender Mütter und Väter* (Union of Single Mothers and Fathers), is as much an organisation for single parents as one predominantly of them. Self-help here is more akin to pressure groups and community organisations within the British voluntary sector.

The idea that empowerment is something that social workers and social work managers should have as a starting point for social work practice seems to have little resonance in the German social work debate. There it is much more about the support social workers should be giving to self-help groups: the principle of *Hilfe zur Selbsthilfe* as described in the publications of the *Arbeitsgemeinschaft der Sozialhilfeinitiativen* (Association of Self-Help Initiatives).

It is not that empowerment is unimportant for clients, but rather that it is the specialist projects and the political system that should be doing it. The specialist organisations for single parents, the social organisations of Turkish migrants, the support projects for drug abusers, and the crisis-point social housing projects use the language of participation. It is not used much elsewhere. However, it is located within the structures and systems of welfare organisation and within the political parties, in particular the Greens. It is noticeable in the radical journals such as *Schwarz auf Weiss: Ihr gutes Recht!* that the policies of the Greens are discussed as important parts of a strategy to promote greater involvement of all people in social welfare issue.

An interesting aside is the worry that some social workers in Germany (and indeed in France) have about 'clientisation': that is, the process of turning people into clients, dependent on social work activities. In discussion this was often referred to as a growing problem, which arises from the great number of social workers who are trained and who need employment. There has been a mushrooming of special projects, all employing social workers, and certainly some are concerned about this trend, which appears to be about protecting social workers' jobs rather than supporting people to set up their own self-help groups.

The user groups that are established in Germany tend to be concerned with participating in the process of negotiating welfare services locally. Charitable and statutory organisations need to determine both the local needs and the ways in which resources are to be spent to meet them, and it is here that self-help groups participate. This is where power lies, and the overriding importance of social planning and social organisation in Germany means that many of the most powerful voices and the people with the highest qualifications can be found in this area. Social planning and coordination are, in many ways, seen as the apogee of the profession of social work. Access to this, rather than to the practice of social work, is therefore the aim of participation. Local committees and local self-help groups know that this is how to get their voices heard.

In Germany most services are provided by voluntary organisations, and local boards will have on them not only the self-help groups but also representatives of users of services. So, as was illustrated in Chapter 4, services for children with disabilities will be provided through local committees which will have on them parents, some young people, local dignitaries, and the representatives of the local charitable bodies. People using such services will not be outside society, but very much part of it, even though the relationship is a dependent one.

The less 'popular' social needs – homelessness, alcohol abusers and single parents – are likely to be helped to set up self-help groups, and to compete with other charitable bodies for funds. Those who are not provided for by the charitable bodies or who do not organise their own self-help groups, and those who receive services unwillingly or who are too disadvantaged to be able to set up their own self-help groups, are outside this. Any broader notion of participation (say, in terms of case conferences, or joint writing of records) seems very little developed, except in a few radical projects.

User participation in management is an increasingly important debate in British social work, but it has not yet gained the weight that it has in Germany. Britain's very different system, where much of the responsibility for the priorities and delivery of services remains with the elected members of a social services committee, means that representation is a very different issue.

One way in which the debate about user participation has emerged in Britain has been through the use of language. This debate exists in Germany, but not to such a great extent. There is a debate about calling people consumers, citizens and residents which reflects as much the different forms in which social care and assistance is given. On the whole the term *Klient* remains in common use, though with apologies. It is only in the more radical journals such as *LAG* (*Ländersarbeitsgemeinschaft Soziale Brennpunkte Hessen*: an organisation of regional workers in 'flashpoint' areas) that the most common alternative term, *Betroffener*, is regularly used. This is usually translated as claimant, but also has the meaning of someone who has been affected by, or has been on the receiving end of, something rather unpleasant.

It has been argued that the absence of a broad-based debate about empowerment is because people know what social workers do, both in terms of remit and skill. A review of the professional press suggested very little debate about the value base of social work intervention, and the remit of social workers. Concerns seem to be much more about the methodologies, the context and the development of strategies of intervention. As services are organised in discrete bodies, each concerned with practical assistance or specialised client support, there is a clear distinction between those who decide that a service or intervention is necessary (e.g. the youth office), and those who provide the social care (generally the voluntary organisations).

Certainly many social workers concerned with making the difficult decisions of, say, removing a child, have described their role, in these situations, as being clearly that of 'social police'. This meant that it was scarcely the sort of service in which many clients would want to participate. Rights are an important issue for social workers, but they are the rights of ensuring due process and justice. Those who delivered the service, even where it was an unwelcome one, felt that their distance from the decision to involve the client in the social control system limited their concern to the provision of services effectively and with dignify. However, even in that user participation was not a great issue.

Within Britain there has been a growing movement to persuade local authorities to provide information on what they do, the criteria for allocating services, and the priorities for receiving them. It has been argued that one of the basic consumerist principles which underlies any promotion of choice must be the provision of information. Information also underlies empowerment. The information that German clients or users have seems to be intended to help them choose between providers of services, and also to help them understand the limits of a social workers' remit.

The belief in the major consumerist demand, that of the right to choose between different services and different providers of service, is very strong in Germany. Although it is clearly a myth for many of the service recipients, particularly the involuntary ones, there is a fairly strong belief that choice is enshrined in the system, and that it ensures that if clients are not happy with the service they receive then they can go elsewhere. In some services, in some regions, there is some truth in this. Charitable bodies compete actively for the contracts to provide popular services, paid for by the *Länder* or the *Bundesrepublik*. The fairly generous amounts of financial assistance for people with physical disabilities does also put some consumer control in the hands of disabled people or their relatives.

Social workers and the skills of participation

The job of a social worker in Britain has been about poverty, inequality, disadvantage and injustice. It has focused on preventive and statutory work in relation to mental health, disability, care of the elderly, and child protection. Although it includes practical help together with moral support, it is not in general concerned with financial support. In Germany, on the other hand, it is about these same aspects of practical support and disadvantage, but it also extends to financial assistance.

The welfarism of Britain includes a broad interpretation of the social worker's role, though with a narrow sector of the population. The view that the state should provide is more all-embracing in Britain than the expectation of welfare interventions in Germany. Although the dependency culture may be a myth, there is still a feeling in the UK that clients need to be empowered against the state. In Germany there is moral panic about neither dependency nor the need to break away from an overpowering 'nanny' state. The debate, as we have seen, is about helping to obtain for local self-help groups and communities greater access to the powerful committees.

It is noticeable that the main critique of the social services system in both Germany and Britain comes mainly from within the profession, not primarily from the users. There are criticisms in what was West Germany from the political right which is concerned with what it sees as increasing stateism. Despite services being delivered by the voluntary sector, their high cost and their increasing appearance as quasi-state agencies lead some to criticise the interventionist role of the state, and lead also to a view that the traditional role of the family is being undermined. A recent conference (1989) held by the DPWV on *Selbsthilfe – Bilanz und Perspektiven* (self-help – taking stock and points of view) had as a major subject the principle of subsidiarity. There were certainly some voices concerned that the principle was being lost.

In Britain many groups and individuals are *not* dealt with by social workers and social work agencies. Homeless people, those in bad housing and those with social education needs or psychological problems are considered to be outside the remit of most social workers. Issues of migration and immigration, women's concerns, debt and financial advice, even welfare rights advice, all tend to be picked up by specialist projects, usually in the voluntary sector. These are all areas in which social workers may be employed, but the workers tend not to use that title. If someone wanting help in any of these areas came to a social services department, they might receive some initial advice but they would usually be referred elsewhere. Much of the work of German social workers happens in such projects dealing with these problems. These would be based in the voluntary sector, or be specialised state projects; the staff would generally have a social work training and describe themselves as social workers.

From the viewpoint of British social workers there is a question about whether the work done by these organisations is indeed social work. In Germany, whatever title is used for the project, the staff are clear that they are social workers and, as has been said earlier, describe their jobs in relation to a knowledge base. Their training and skills are those of social workers, the application of which may be useful in a number of settings. This is much more common in Germany where social services planning and research officers will describe themselves (because of their original training) as, for example, sociologists.

These differences are almost certainly a reflection of the two education and training traditions. Although its training has grown out of both the social administration and pschodynamic traditions, British social work has always felt a little uneasy in its claim to have its own body of knowledge. German training has, on the other hand, been taught through an emphasis on technical theory which has acknowledged discrete areas of knowledge and particular skills to be the basis of social work interventions.

Social work in Britain is often described as a value-based profession, and certainly the words that social workers use to describe their activities are those of abstract values such as empowerment, protection, participation and equality. German social workers, on the other hand, more commonly talk about social work as being a knowledge-based profession, and talk about their activities in terms of socialisation, changing behaviour and offering advice. This distinction may reinforce the sense that in Germany it is more generally understood what social workers do as regards both their remit and their limits.

This difference affects the way in which social workers might involve the recipients of services in negotiating social work interventions. If participation and empowerment are amongst the basic goals of social work, demonstrating greater personal functioning, then of course participative practices are essential. If, though, social workers are fairly certain that they hold a body of expertise that can help people to socialise more effectively, then it is not likely that participation in professional practice and methods is very welcome, or even very productive. Participation in terms of information and choice to help people resolve their problems in their own ways may be more relevant.

Participation in Germany, then, is seen to be important in terms of the organisation and the structure, but not the method of intervention or the professional methodology. These are not conceptualised as negotiable in the way they are in Britain. They are seen as a more clearly distinct group of skills and methods which the social worker will apply, in a situation where their skills will be acknowledged.

The involvement of the organisation may be negotiable, and indeed the social worker may therefore be more vulnerable in terms of security of employment. Once the particular organisation and staff have taken on the tasks, their skills are assumed to be accepted and understood, more like any other professional.

Participation: social work or social action?

At the beginning of this chapter we considered whether it should, in the British sense, be social workers or some other professional or occupational group that should be the practitioners of participation.

There has been in Britain a long and political battle between two schools of activity, social work and community work. This distinction exists in other European countries, but there is not quite the same separate philosophy or political rhetoric. Many people who work in community and social action programmes of the sort described in earlier chapters would, in Britain, describe themselves as community workers, or perhaps just project workers. There would be less shyness about using the term 'social worker' in many other European countries.

The European programmes and resolutions on social conditions and poverty have been picked up by community workers in Britain, but have not on the whole been seen as relevant by social workers. The European picture is different, and many more people employed in community employment projects, migrancy schemes and training initiatives come from the broad range of social work activity.

It is easier to see how a concern with social education, financial benefits, and socialisation in German social welfare fits more readily into the interests and categories of the EC than do some of the aspects of British social services work. However, the concern with solidarity and integration of disadvantaged communities would certainly fit into the value systems of much of British social work. One reason that the EC may feel irrelevant to British social workers is the way EC client groups are described (see Chapters 1 and 7). These are generally in employment and labour market terms, and are not usually how British social workers tend to describe their services or client groups. These labels do, however, fit in more with the language and organisation of community work.

In Chapter 1 there was a discussion about recapturing a lost role for social work in Britain. The current review of the British welfare state, the moves towards greater plurality, to using the strengths of the community, and to encouraging preventive work may mean that, together with the influence of greater Europeanisation, it does just that.

The idea of solidarity is very important in the European ideal, along with subsidiarity. Participation is about mutual responsibility and, in these terms, the ideas of subsidiarity and solidarity, integration and self-help, may come to have an increasing effect on British social work.

Within this there is a role for British social work: it may be a very pragmatic one, relating more to the broader concepts that underpin the European vision than to any one specific programme. But even within the limitations of the EC's structures there are considerable opportunities for pursuing some of the shared goals of participation, of promoting rights and justice, that are so vital to social work values and practices.

In the next chapter we shall examine some of the rhetoric and reality of the European social vision, and consider whether its agenda will be beneficial for the future role of social work.

7

Social Europe, Social Action and Social Work

'It is really quite simple. We say that 1992 must not be just about business and profit but about the ordinary people – the citizens and the workers – who make the Community what it is.'
(Matthias Hinterscheid, General Secretary, European Trade Union Confederation, at a rally of pensioners and trade unionists to demand the implementation of the Social Charter, Brussels, 1990)

British social work in the 1980s and 1990s

British social work is going through a period of considerable uncertainty. It is searching for new purpose and a new theoretical base. The argument of this book is that a clear involvement with European social action agendas can give it that purpose, and that the experience and traditions of other forms of social work can be useful in creating that new theoretical base. At this time of uncertainty, the realisation of closer involvement with European institutions and practices offers an opportunity to think again about the present state of British social work, and a chance to change direction. There is a feeling that the 1980s were a pretty grim decade for British social work: a European perspective may help us identify what that new direction might be.

The current dilemma of social work is shown in the contrast between the professional debate about its purpose, and its popular image. The language social work uses to describe itself is broadly that of consumerism or of empowerment. The public view of it is one of child-snatchers and well-meaning but ineffectual social police.

British social work is in a sorry state, depressed, unable to articulate a positive image of itself, defensive and undervalued. At the same time it is more talked about and argued about than at almost any other time in its history.

Social work has been seen by its practitioners as a positive and vital activity undertaken by people committed to improving the social and living conditions of those in poverty and distress. This focus has been lost as it has been used increasingly as a social police force, trying to maintain order amongst the uncertain consequence of economic and political changes. In Britain social workers have become the whipping boys of structural change, blamed not only for the dependency alleged to have resulted from the growth of the welfare state, but also the personal chaos that occurs in individual lives.

We have seen that the picture of social work throughout Europe is one of having to get to grips with industrial and economic restructuring. However, in our partner countries it has not always led to such an emphasis on either the individual or on social control. Rather it has also promoted social and collective action, often supported by the programmes of the EC.

We shall examine later what the effects of the EC have been and could be for British and European social work, but first let us briefly examine some of the factors that have influenced British social work recently. This will form a backdrop to the debate on Europe.

In Britain the emphasis has been not on the collective but on the individual and on a crisis-dominated approach to social work. During the 1970s and 1980s social work established itself in the social services and social work departments of local authorities. Child-care legislation and the public concern with child-care scandals dominated their development.

By the late 1970s and throughout the 1980s this particular focus coincided with a battle between the interests of local and central government. Despite the rhetoric, the conflict was not solely about the levels of public spending, or the creation of local accountability and democracy. However, the consequence of these skirmishes was a constant squeeze on the resources available to local government. Whatever plans it had for urban regeneration, for developing rural networks, for developing the isolated estates and new towns, were lost. They were deemed to be expressions of collectivism and undue state interference at a time when individuals were expected to pull themselves and their families into prosperity. Anything else looked like socialism and this, like 'society', was not on the agenda. At this time some social work practitioners were putting themselves even further out on a limb by promoting the ideas of community social work and decentralisation. It was not an auspicious time to urge a new confidence in social work.

The expansion of local government that had characterised much of the 1960s and 1970s came to an abrupt end as the recession of the 1980s took hold. The limited resources of local government became overstretched in trying to deal with the consequences of a halt in capital expenditure, the decline in local infrastructure and the limitation of local spending to the policies of a lick and a promise. Local councils quite simply did what they could, but largely only what they must.

For social work this has been disastrous. Most social work activity took place within these generic, but child-care dominated, social work departments. In the minds of the public, and of many social workers, social work became synonymous with child abuse and child protection work. At the same time social work began to re-emerge in sectors other than local government. The expectations of the Seebohm (1968), Barclay (1982) and Wagner (1988) reviews of social work services had been that most social work would take place within a local authority context. These ideas were beached on the central-government-inspired sands of restricted public spending, pluralism and the mixed economy, and a belief in the need to support the individual, not society.

At first much of the social work profession was left behind by the growth of pluralism. Whilst social workers were defending their services against cuts, the private sector, supported by central government, made a foray into the provision of residential care for elderly people. It did not last, rising and falling with the level of government subsidies. The voluntary sector, meanwhile, began pitching for the new contracts to run community care and mental health establishments in the wake of the closure of psychiatric hospitals. Most of all, the users of services themselves began to give voice, demanding involvement in the creation of care plans and representation in decision-making. They said forcefully that local authorities had not always been responsive, listened to their complaints, or given them respect. Now they wanted to use social workers differently, as advocates and advisors, not as their guardians (Beresford and Croft, 1986; Berry and Doyle, 1989).

All of these changes led social workers to become less and less certain about their professional purpose, and even that their 'natural' place of employment was in the social services department. It certainly reinforced a retreat into a more limited concern: the social care and protection of those at risk. The social action of the 1960s was replaced by a view of social workers as social police. The image of the radical social worker who set up welfare rights projects on impoverished estates was replaced by a bogey figure who, like the NSPCC officer of old, was concerned only with 'cruelty', though in its modern guise of abuse.

Finally, there is the family. In policy terms, the 1980s were the years of the family as the source of comfort and succour. No longer could people rely on the support of society; it had apparently disappeared. The family had become the acknowledged provider of social support. This could be through changing social security arrangements so that young people had to rely on their families to support them financially, or through an emphasis on the family as the place for the social care of elderly or disabled relatives.

Whilst putting this often unbearable strain on families, there was a concurrent concern with those that were seen as dysfunctional. Those that did not function well enough were subject to an unprecedented level of scrutiny and policing. Family centres were intended to support those with minor problems, and instead were faced with more serious family breakdown or disadvantage (Cannan 1992), evidenced by child abuse and ritual abuse, as these became a public obsession. As a result, the public was both supportive of social work involvement and highly critical of it.

All this has led to a major and dramatic uncertainty for social work, both in its focus and in terms of the sectors in which it should take place. Our contention is that Europe can create the framework for a more positive and creative view of social work; one which cares for the individual, but within a wider social and community context. We also contend that the tradition of social action and community support in the EC and the other European countries could help to create a relevant methodology and ideology for British social work.

In this chapter we shall examine the joint social agendas of Europe and social work, and the social actions that have emerged to create a new future for European and British social work. Despite the view of many commentators that Europe will be solely an economic entity, the strength of the themes we identified at the beginning of this book reinforce our view that Europe will continue to have a social dimension, and that this dimension will be increasingly important for British, as well as European, social work.

Social action has been placed firmly on the agenda of the EC, and indeed the Commission. However some fear that membership of Europe, particularly because of the presence of the poorer 'peripheral' nations, will instead mean that the welfare philosophies will be regarded as too generous and too expensive, and will be quietly dropped. However, this is unlikely. Most of the original signatories of the European Economic Union are the same countries as those that have invested over a century of energy, debate and resources in creating welfare systems. This history will probably ensure that the EC remains a means of relieving, or at least containing, the new poverty and marginalisation within Europe. They are, of course, likely to try to find a form of welfare which relates to their current economic means. Welfare has always followed the demands of economics and the rhetoric of democracy. In this final chapter we shall chart some of its current path.

The joint agenda of social work and social Europe

In the first chapter we saw how the idea of *l'espace social* became a battleground on which the two contenders, freedom from regulation and interference on the one side, and the growth of European powers to direct and create social protection on the other, have sometimes clashed. It has also been the focus for a conflict between individual and collective responses to social problems. The poverty programmes, for example, have contrasted the effects of individual, social case-work responses with collective and organised actions. Influenced by the French philosophy of *insertion* (see Chapter 5), the EC has furthered attempts to frame some newer policies which balance regulation and protection with individual freedom.

Social action and intervention have been the main platforms of the EC's strategy for the implementation of social policy. These programmes and initiatives, although involving relatively few people and communities, have tended to use the methods and activities of classic social development. As these techniques have been more commonly used to articulate opposition to state actions this has resulted in a rather uneasy relationship between the European state and local communities. However, many are beginning to acknowledge a mutual benefit.

As the histories of social welfare were reviewed in Chapter 2, we saw how models had been adapted to meet the changing political and economic needs of the different countries during industrialisation and after the Second World War. More recently the models have changed again in response to the new mass migration, to racism and to women's expectations of involvement in the labour force, making them less available to be the main providers of welfare.

Since the 1970s all the European countries have debated what has felt like a crisis of welfare. This crisis is perceived to be caused by high spending on social security, social mobility and the breakdown of traditional family support. This has resulted in a fundamental rethinking of the role and locus of social work interventions. The language of pluralism, and of balancing solidarity and subsidiarity, has come to have increased importance in determining the next stages of welfare. As we reviewed the activities and functions of social work within the various countries in Chapter 3, a number of themes emerged. For example, despite the different means of organising and financing social work, they all have in common a concern to tackle not only the effects but also the cause of social disadvantage. The systems, to varying degrees, also promote advocacy and support so that people can receive much-needed social services, and also have their voices heard somewhere in the decision-making processes. Although the client groups are much the same in each country, there have been trends within these which have meant different problems have been prioritised, and different solutions found. For example, child abuse work became significant in Britain in the late 1960s and 1970s, but only became a major issue in France and West Germany in the 1980s.

Similarly, work with unemployed young people from migrant and minority ethnic groups became a political priority in many countries during the 1980s in response to urban unrest. However, the responses in some countries were integrated firmly into employment and work programmes, whereas in others they were part of education projects to teach social and personal development skills. Chapter 4 analysed these responses in relation to different countries' histories and traditions.

The unified approach in France to programmes of social integration and personal development harks back to the origins of social work in Britain, when social case work and social reform were closely aligned. Recently the more campaigning aspects of social work have become separated into two traditions in Britain, those of social work and community work. The European programmes have begun to create a common language and common set of objectives in which each of these traditions may find a role. This could make social workers the practitioners of participation. Chapter 6 showed how these policies of participation have gone hand in hand with initial steps to create citizens' rights for users of social welfare.

These policies of *insertion* and integration have an obvious political purpose within the Community. As its borders are redefined there needs to be a stability and sense of common interest for those within them. At the same time there is a need to diffuse the potential social unrest and insecurity that could result from the enormous political and economic re-structuring that Europe is undergoing.

To conclude this study we shall examine again some of the aims of Europe and of social work, and consider what effects each could have on the other's agenda.

The joint agenda: protection and integration

Both social work and social Europe share a concern to pro-tect the vulnerable and to integrate people through social action into a wider community of interest. Within the Com-mission of the EC the view is beginning to take hold that the integrated market can only be justified in terms of increased social progress (Hayward, 1990). A document of the Com-mission of the EC, Social Europe: 'Social Dimensions of the Internal Market', put it like this: 'the internal Market must be conceived in such a manner as to benefit all our people' (Commission of the EC, 1988). Although the themes of citizenship, integration and the protection of vulnerable people are common to the European vision and to European social work, a social dimension is going to be even more difficult to achieve than is developing a single economic market.

As we have seen, social work organisations and remits are based on deep-rooted ideological and moral values which have created the different forms of welfare that we have observed in each country. Despite the great emphasis on the new economic rhetoric of welfare, of consumerism and plu-ralism, people have fundamental expectations of welfare serv-ices, how they are structured and how they are delivered. Market forces may not be enough to challenge these.

The rhetoric and the reality

Before getting too carried away by the joint agendas of social work and social Europe, it is worth sounding a note of caution. The European ideal is of an end to marginalisation for the dispossessed, charters of rights for those who receive services, and participation in decision-making for the users of services. However, little in recent experience, despite the excellence of many of the European programmes (and indeed the exchanges that have gone on between the different countries), has led us to feel that the reality will match up. We have heard the rhetoric of integration, but current statements are beginning to suggest that there is a growing tension between this and the reinforcement of marginalisation.

Evan as the Community has developed programmes to tackle social marginalisation and vulnerability, it has spent far more time, and much more of its financial power and resources, on developing programmes which have done the reverse (Jarré, 1990).

The language and rhetoric of the EC may itself cause some initial problems. In Britain we have tended to use words such as self-help and mutual support, participation and disadvantage to describe social work's interests. They may mean similar things, but they have a very different feel about them. As we begin, rather self-consciously to use the language of solidarity, subsidiarity and marginalisation we may find that we change the way in which we conceptualise social problems, and therefore the models of welfare that we adopt to try to resolve them. Already we can see the British system of state provision giving way to one in which a mixed economy of provision and new partnerships are being formed. Language may lead us into still more debate. However, we need to be wary of a too-easy assumption that the vocabulary is heralding a new world of social equality. Marginalisation may just be Euro-speak for stigma, and social action may reinforce this, substituting work with one group of margainalised people for another, replacing the stigmatisation of individuals with that of whole communities.

On the other hand, the changed vocabulary may have other effects. If the terms marginalisation and solidarity are used to describe the objectives of social policy, it could result in a changed perception of the clients of social work practice. This could be very effective in changing the view of clients from an individualised and privatised one to one in which the dignity and rights of citizens are acknowledged. Such a change could be as significant as the shift from the vocabulary of deserving and undeserving poor, from treatment and rehabilitation, to rights and responsibilities, to users and citizens.

In addition, a new understanding of the implications of marginalisation could bring about the pragmatic recognition that the stability of any community is not improved if it excludes large numbers of its citizens. Again, though, the social agendas of Europe, despite the rhetoric, have continued to emphasise the difference between in- and outsiders. To some extent this is unsurprising: any market needs to be concerned with its borders, and those within and without them. However, the radical changes in Eastern Europe have demonstrated very starkly the difficulties facing the EC, as these economically underdeveloped countries have tried to gain admission. The poorer countries and regions of the Mediterranean, and the peripheral regions of parts of Scotland, Ireland, and parts of Germany and France, have already caused the central zones and countries considerable concern. How many poor countries can be allowed to join this economic and social union if the cost will be a reduction of living standards for the wealthy? When the poor regions were in a minority then the wealthy countries encouraged solidarity with the poorer ones. Marginalisation was a problem of the few to be tackled by the many.

Now that the new applicants are countries that have been wholly marginalised, and the recession of the late 1980s has bitten harder, it has become a less welcome proposition. Indeed, it is being asked: will the poorer countries wish to join if the EC is no longer a rich countries' club?

There is a growing paradox in Europe, as the barriers are being lifted and national frontiers are disappearing; instead of a widening of horizons many people are becoming more chauvinistic and nationalistic. Racism is growing and fear is beginning to dominate European policy. In particular fears are growing of the arrival of potentially millions of economic refugees: migrant workers with a right to stay and to receive housing, work and social care. There is a likelihood that Europe will become less concerned with the politics of cooperation and unity, as it balances the competing needs of old and new members. As has been said about the new Germany, reunification is driving a wedge between us (Marsh, 1991).

The integration of the agendas: the new challenges for social work

The challenge to incorporate a European dimension into social work is one in which practitioners and policy-makers are engaged in the different member states. At the same time the EC is addressing itself to the means by which its social policies can be implemented through these practitioners of participation. Although it is hard to identify all the effects of a European consciousness on social work, we can begin to look at the influence on the framework in which it operates: its organisation, its workforce, its practices and indeed its choice of clients. We can also begin to see how social work and social action could influence the European debate, and begin to suggest actions that can be undertaken so that European social workers, in Britain and elsewhere, can influence the policies that will be developed to manage the changes in European society.

The framework for social interventions

On the whole the programmes of the Commission have developed responses to social need based on a concept of vulnerability. This could provide a framework for social action which could be very 'social-work friendly'. Beresford Hayward, an EC adviser looking at the development of its programmes, has shown that the emphasis of the Commission has been on individuals and groups who have been identified as 'vulnerable' within a free market economy (Hayward, 1990). It has also recognised that there are likely to be more such people in the new, post-1992 open-bordered Common Market. Thus the Commission's Social Action Programmes address such areas of concern as elderly people, disadvantaged youth, urban and rural poverty, drugs, AIDS and the family.

Many of these are the target groups of much social work intervention. Looking again at the basic assumptions of the European social programmes we can see an intention to develop people so that they become less vulnerable, and more able to confront particularly difficult periods of their lives. However, it has been argued by Hayward (1991) that in creating these programmes, the EC has not sufficiently drawn out the aspects that relate to the way in which social problems are usually conceptualised within the different welfare systems. He has argued that the Commission needs a more conscious focus to ensure the role of the programmes in social participation is emphasised, and not just their role in economic integration. Many of the programmes could be repackaged, and Hayward has examined the programmes to see how they relate to the development of vulnerable people and social participation.

The needs of children and the family have been seen to be important to many of the social action programmes (European Observatory on National Family Policies, EC, 1989a). Measures to assure women's participation in the economy, such as the creation of high standards of child care, training, job access and protection, can be seen to have social development objectives, not just those of economic integration. Anti-poverty programmes, employment training for young people and for adults with disabilities have similarly generally been described in terms of the promotion of effective employment policies for the economy. However, they obviously have a more social role. This has come to be recognised in projects concerning people with disabilities, for example, or from minority ethnic groups which have applied for funds. Many have become skilled in repackaging their aims and objectives to fit the overt requirements. If social action were to become an explicit aim of the Community then such convoluted games playing could be avoided and more groups might have the confidence to apply for funding (Euromonitor, 1990). It is not such a huge step for the Commission to recognise social goals in its action programmes, or for social work to repackage its concerns into those of the Community: 'Making this linkage more explicit could show the way to a workable framework, anchoring the many objectives of these programmes to a common fundamental outcome' (Hayward, 1990).

Social and community programmes to create self-esteem, social capacity and a sense of involvement are also necessary. Currently these are seen as a by-product of policies to promote reintegration to the labour market. If the logic of the 'social charter' were taken as a base then this could be turned on its head. The social programmes to create integration into the workforce could address the experience of vulnerability, and new training programmes could go far beyond the practical skills of the job. Similar connections could be made with other programmes: those for poverty, women, immigrants, youth training and intergenerational solidarity all demonstrate the ways in which these policies, which are ostensibly for economic integration, could be seen to have a clear social action and social work agenda. They are all concerned to promote the conditions in which human potential can be achieved, and the well-being of individuals within society.

The objectives of such programmes are not always easily achieved. For example, a programme for drug abusers demonstrated the problems of promoting social solidarity for people who are often stigmatised and rejected by society. For it to succeed it depended upon intervention on both a communal and an individual basis, with collaboration between health, social, employment and other services. However, the programme was promoted as one which enable vulnerable people to return to the employment market. Despite this emphasis, its activities do not suggest this was its sole objective (Hayward, 1990).

It is, of course, important to see that the arguments for programmes are indeed based on the political and economic agendas, but they are also firmly intended to have a social element. Social integration is essential for political and economic stability, but it is also a goal in itself, and one which could be better exploited in partnership with social work objectives. If the EC were to 'sell' its programmes in a different way then its concerns and priorities could become an exciting framework for social action and social work in Europe, and specifically in Britain.

The organisational context

In earlier chapters we have seen that major differences exist between the organisation and management of social work in Britain and the rest of Europe. However, this is in no way a static picture, and as Britain develops a more pluralist structure for social services delivery it has a profile which is increasingly European. This is not surprising. Social policy and social work have been shaped by industrial development and the needs of the economy, by demographic trends and the ideologies and political clout of influential groups such as the Church. There is now an additional force, European membership and the Community Charter of Social Rights for Workers (the Social Charter).

The market and pluralistic social economies of our partners have encouraged a debate about the creation of a welfare society and not a welfare state. Britain may begin to review the assumptions that have been made about the proper role of the state. It is no longer quite so obvious that the state should be the main provider of social care, and that the other sectors should have only a residual or supplementary role. Indeed, many of the other European models imply a residual role for the state, and also that the voluntary and not for profit sectors should have a dominant role. This debate has not only come about because of a wish to embrace the market, but also because of dissatisfaction with state provision.

As we have seen, the British scene is changing rapidly. Even the churches are now gaining a significant role in the delivery of social care, particularly amongst the minority ethnic communities who feel that the British state has ignored their cultural and religious needs.

The expectation of the community care legislation and the Children Act, 1989, is that local authorities will increasingly take on an enabling role. Partnerships with and support for the independent sector is now an expectation of government. That the local state has provided so much of the service delivery is inconceivable to many other European nations; it may be becoming inconceivable in Britain, too.

As the EC has embraced the principle of subsidiarity to limit the undue influence of the state in individual's lives, it may be that there will be a greater degree of service provision by the independent sector. This has to remain a highly contentious aspect of European social policy. However, as even Sweden (not yet an EC country) elected a government in 1991 which wished to dismantle the welfare state, the tide may have turned against the predominance of state provision. It should not be thought that this is necessarily the same as losing state funding for social welfare. Another message from our European partners and from the EC itself is that social policy and social spending are of considerable importance in the social and economic welfare of their countries, and state support and resourcing for welfare is essential.

The workforce of social action: social workers or other professionals?

Many of the target groups of EC policy are the same as those of social work intervention. However, in the same way as the programmes have not been packaged to emphasise their relevance to social work, neither have they been addressed to social workers. This is surprising, especially as we have already seen that social workers have in many contexts become the practitioners of participation. The French, for example, have used social workers in programmes to tackle exclusion (see Chapter 5). Within a European context, though, there has not been a targeting of social workers as the workforce of the social action programmes, or at least not in the way in which Britain uses the term. The workforce has more often been called project workers or, more commonly, community workers. This is in itself one of the reasons why British social work has been so little affected by the programmes of the

EC. The limited job title may have limited activities so that projects have been outside the mainstream of social work and social work departments.

Community workers and special project workers in Britain have, however, made considerable use of the opportunities to promote their work in the European context, even managing to get a resolution passed to promote the funding and use of community work within the activities of the EC (Resolution 208, 1989). Within the voluntary sector the emphasis of the European initiatives has not seemed so alien. Many of the major voluntary organisations, particularly the community work ones such as the Community Development Foundation, have been active not only in gaining access to EC money for these programmes but also in promoting to practitioners a sense of the importance of European links. Voluntary sector organisations, such as the National Children's Bureau, the Volunteer Centre, Community Service Volunteers and Age Concern have all engaged in European activities for over a decade, involving not only their policy staff but also their practitioners.

These developments have not been so common in the statutory sector, and certainly EC-inspired activities have been peripheral to the main statutory work of social services departments. There has not been any real lead from the Department of Health, other than in connection with the development of legislation promoting clients' access to records. Even this has been somewhat grudgingly given. This may change if the more pro-European statements of the current Conservative government turn into national policy initiatives.

It is not only Britain that may need to rethink the role and title of social workers. As a united Europe begins to focus on social action on poverty, integration and citizenship, there may be wider encouragement of a review of their training, status and functions. This has been shown in different ways: there is a debate current in the former West Germany about whether the term *sozialarbeiter* (social worker) should be dropped in favour of the more generic term *sozialpädagoge* in recognition of their increased emphasis on socialisation and integration. We can already see in Britain one new type of worker, the case manager, who may not be (by training or title) a social worker, but who will certainly perform many of the tasks of assessment, case planning and allocation of resources that have been associated with British social work. They are also the tasks of many social workers in other countries. This may be the beginning of the movement to realign some of the activities of social workers into new moulds. This process may continue as other types of social worker emerge.

Residential care workers may have their work and activities realigned to more common European standards as, for example, the charters of rights of users become more influential. Reference has already been made to the hybrid task of social development workers, taking on something of the *sozialpädagoge* and something of the *animateur*, together with the social worker. A real challenge for the social work profession in Britain will be its ability to undertake the broader roles of workers within society, concerned with social integration and community involvement. There is already a basis for this in community social work, and the opening of doors as demanded by the reports of Wagner and Barclay. Indeed social work has an older tradition of being the active supporter of the poor and the excluded, and the advocate of the marginalised, whether they be poor, disabled, elderly or homeless.

This objective of developing society, and not only the individual, could and should be revived. If nothing else this is the point of our enthusiasm for Europe. It should be a rallying cry for calls to better the conditions of people outside the current, rather narrow, concerns of social work. They may not immediately attract funding from the central or local state, but as they fit with the priorities of Europe, broaden their focus and the places in which they are undertaken, then they may receive European backing.

This, if the emphasis on marginalisation, exclusion and integration does become important, could be the exciting future for the European social work profession.

Social work's practices and clients

If we can suggest that Europe has affected the organisation, framework and profession of social work, then it should also be possible to identify some possible effects on practice. It has to be said this is less clear. However, it certainly has had an impact at an ideological level. As there is more discussion of the Social Charter, as the concept of rights and the enforcement of these through social contracts becomes more current, this will begin to affect the social work practice of individual practitioners. Some social work policies, such as the closing down of large psychiatric hospitals in Italy, and the promotion of community care packages in France and Britain, have been influenced by these ideas. However, the development of charters of rights and contracts between social workers and clients have come about not only because of this European ideal. Pressure groups of many social workers in Europe have also been behind this, as professional practice has absorbed new ideas and values in line with the growth of democratic pluralism. Being a member of a wider community and being open to new ideas may in itself have as much effect on practice. How far these cross-fertilisations develop will probably depend more on the growing number of exchanges of professionals and students, the international conferences and the professional links that are made, than on any direct lead from Europe. Of course, some of these have been funded by EC initiatives. Many more have developed through other networks, chance contacts, and the enthusiasm of key individuals and associations (Cannan, Coleman and Lyons, 1990).

At a broader level, social work practice will be influenced by the recommendations of the Committee of Ministers at the Council of Europe on, for example, the role, training and status of social workers (Resolution (67)16), on social and medico-social policy for old age (Resolution (70)16), and on the social services for physically or mentally handicapped persons (Resolution (973)1). These may begin to affect not only the context within which social work interventions are made, but also the actions themselves. However, the effects on practice of such resolutions have so far been limited.

The Commission has not been much more successful in having a direct influence on practice. For many years DG5 has been publishing reports of case studies and comparative interventions which could have led to changed ideas. Amongst these have been 'Social action to prevent the breakdown of the family, the neglect of children and juvenile delinquency' (1972); 'Social measures regarding the placing of children in community homes or foster families' (1973); 'The causes and prevention of child abuse' (1979); and 'The Council of Europe and child welfare – the need for a European convention of Children's Rights' (1990).

Furthermore, Europe as an entity has not been seen to have much to offer directly to practitioners. To counterbalance this, there is another tradition, much older than the EC: that of Western European countries learning from each other. We have already seen how the pension reforms of Bismarck in the late nineteenth century were influential in many countries; the development of high standards of care in residential and day care organisation promoted by the private organisations of the former West Germany, and the treatment of young offenders and drug abusers in the Netherlands, have all had their imitators and followers in other countries. Conductive education is a current example of a practice that has no geographical boundaries either for the providers of the services or for its users. However, there has not yet been that much interest in looking at Europe as an entity to get new ideas of practice and methodologies. Certainly in Britain we have been far more influenced by American traditions and practices than by our European neighbours.

This may be changing, as the influence of the ERASMUS programme and, even more practically, the need to regulate and register the profession of social work, its professional standards, training and forms of accountability, begin to have an effect. In particular the directive on training for professions, with an expectation of three years of higher education, may eventually raise the academic status of social work training or, if this is not achieved, may marginalise it in Britain. It is ironic, given the interest in Europe in social work courses, that the British government's stance on the length of qualifying education should be so out of step with our partners.

The new models that are emerging for social work practice build on the traditions of community and solidarity. They have as their base a respect for human rights, social justice, and hearing the voices of the user. They acknowledge the skills and expertise of professional social workers, but recognise that theirs is the difficult task of balancing individual freedoms with social protection and responsibilities.

Social workers in many countries have felt undervalued and out of kilter with policy makers. Although it is not a cure-all, the rhetoric of Europe could give weight to social work's concerns to value all individuals and communities within societies, not just the economically successful.

Making social workers' voices heard in Europe

We have seen some of the ways in which social work's context, organisation, and practice could be influenced by the experience of a consciousness of Europe, and particularly the EC. Social work can also have its influence in Europe. The social rhetoric of Europe is limited, but it is there. Greater links and greater confidence could make this a reality. We shall look at some ways of gaining these.

Social work networks and their influence in Europe

Social workers tend to be avid networkers, and those who have a strong commitment to Europe have been building up networks both of individuals and of institutions. The National Institute for Social Work in Britain was for many years part of a network of similar institutions in the Netherlands and Belgium which produced research documents, seminars and conference on social development issues. Newer networks, such as ESAN (European Social Action Network), and

Euro-Social Network, alongside older ones such as ESDA (European Social Development Associates) and ECDE (European Community Development Exchange) have been established to exchange information on practice and innovation, and will also become important data bases for knowledge of social affairs in Europe. More formal federations, such as Euro-link Age (for organisations of elderly people) and COFACE (Confederation of Family Organisations in the European Community) already act as invaluable resources for interpreting the EC's policies to social work and voluntary organisations. Through their publications and networks they have had considerable influence on the development of European social policy. ECAS and the European Children's Centre (based at the National Children's Bureau in Britain) are just two of the new organisations that are being established to strengthen the voice of those affected by the social policies of Europe.

Some of these initiatives are working towards the establishment of a formal European Observatory of Social Work Activities. Others wish to gather information and experience to lobby for changed policies and priorities. Some of these bodies have received EC money for start-up conferences, and some receive funding for project work and research. Many more are financed locally and nationally and by the voluntary contributions of their members.

Increasingly the purpose of these networks and bodies has been to ensure that the social action elements of the Social Charter are given prominence in the planning of Europe. To this end networks of the directors of European social work services, of the professional associations of social workers, of social care staff such as home-help organisers, and the professional journals of social work have been established.

More will be formed. They are likely to become an important means of funnelling some of the concerns about the appropriate tasks for social workers in this changing European context. If social work is a negotiated activity it must reflect the changing social context within which it operates. Increasingly this will be both European and very local. It is likely that ideas will change about the focus for social work: occupational social work, work following disasters, the support of migrants and their families; all of these may become, in the British sense, statutory activities as the European Commission and Parliament create new agendas for social intervention. The networks of social action and social development are a very important step towards ensuring that the social concerns of practitioners, managers and trainers of social work are included in the creation of social objectives for Europe. There is currently no formal lobby for social work in Brussels, although there are moves towards establishing one (Jarré, 1990). This will be necessary to ensure that the specific concerns of social work organisations and their staff are recognised. Social work should not have a passive reactive role, but use these networks and organisations to press for its voice to be heard and its influence to be felt.

British social work in the new Europe

Given the uncertainties for British social work that were discussed at the beginning of this chapter, we argue that the added dimension of a European context and a European vision, together with the initiatives of the European Commission, can begin to create a framework of a more optimistic future. The social work profession will need to re-examine its practices and organisation, and to reconsider its place in social action and social concern. This it can do by its bold assertion that not only community but society exists, and by expressing a belief in interventions which lie between solidarity and subsidiarity. There must be a place which offers social care to those who are marginalised; this is essential to the well-being of any society. The European vision may offer a new hope for an end to exclusion from the broader society. The principle of collective social responsibility could emphasise the importance of accountable local intervention. At the same time, the principle of subsidiarity (making those interventions at the nearest possible point to those in need) could well support the moves towards greater plurality, and the need to provide services in a number of different ways. These could be from the state, and the voluntary sector and, now, the private sector.

Most of all, the European emphasis on reintegration and on margainalisation could be seen as invaluable in challenging the stigmatisation of those who receive social work services. Active membership of the EC, embracing a wider European vision, could be the opportunity to re-examine the way in which we see social problems, and the solutions we try. Social Europe gives a context for the ideology of empowerment as a framework for creating practices which tackle oppression. The European ideology gives a context for the policies of equal opportunities, for minority rights, and for promoting minimum standards of social care. This ideology, so close to that of social work, must be an ally in reasserting the confidence of social work in taking its place in social change. More social action programmes could mean, as in France, that social work could itself become a less marginalised profession, more involved in planning at different levels, and more able to work in partnership with other professional and local groups.

However, we should not get carried away with our enthusiasm: there are dangers in the European vision, too. For some it could cause the loss of some of the more individualistic person-centred aspects of social work. Many fear that social work will become the panacea for social insecurity; that the effects of fundamental economic and industrial issues and the consequences of political instability and enormous uncertainty will fall at social work's door.

Furthermore, we can be sure of a few things: the new Europe of the 1990s will see a growth of poverty and of migration. There will be a breakdown of traditional assumptions about family and social support. Racism and exclusion will grow, and civil rights for those who are not welcomed into citizenship within Europe may disappear. In ending one form of exclusion, others will emerge. Social work will need to restate its support for all vulnerable people within the new society.

If social work values and structures mirror the society in which it is undertaken, reflecting economic, demographic, ideological and political imperatives, then it must keep changing. Because it is a locally negotiated activity it must acknowledge the changed expectations and values of that society.

Local and national history has, as we have seen in earlier chapters, a real effect on the form in which social work takes place, the values that inform it, and where it is found. Although the European nations have developed different systems, they have in common a need to combine social aspirations and stability with the changing demands of modernising, urbanising and declining economies.

The new Europe will have yet other preoccupations. As the barriers come down between the member states, and the countries of Eastern Europe and others apply for membership, its economic base will change and it will no longer be a rich countries' club. The probability of migration on a new scale, bringing with it problems of social integration, exclusion and isolation, will challenge its social as well as its geographical boundaries. It may be that this will produce a diverse, energetic, federated union which values difference and can afford to pay for the equal citizenship of all its members. It is equally likely that it will create a great number of marginalised people and that the problems of exclusion will grow; poverty will increase.

At the same time the rhetoric of solidarity and integration, and the ideas of citizenship and participation, will have become part of the united European language. This changed and uncertain history will produce both the demands of new economic relationships, and also the growth of different ideologies. Within this social work will be negotiated. The boundaries of the local community will still be of great importance to social work in each country, but the residents and employers, the planners and the financiers, will develop allegiances which are beyond these, and beyond their separate nations.

Social work's preoccupations must reflect this changing and challenging world to find its new place within social Europe.

Bibliography

Arrouet, A. (1988) *Réseau Lexovien d'Échanges de Savoirs: Evaluation de 1987–88*, Caen, CAF.

Baker, J. (1986) 'Comparing national priorities: family and population policies in Britain and France', *Journal of Social Policy*, 15 (4), pp. 421–41.

Bakker, I. (1988) 'Women's employment in comparative perspective', in J. Jenson, Hagen, E. and Reddy, C. (eds) *Feminization of the Labour Force: Paradoxes and Promises*, Cambridge, Polity.

Barclay, P. (1982) *Social Workers: Their Roles and Tasks*, London, National Institute for Social Work.

Barr, H. (1989a) 'Odd one out', *Community Care*, 20 July.

Barr, H. (1989b) *Social Work Education in its European Context*, London, CCETSW.

Bartlett, N. (1989) 'Caring the French way', *Community Care*, 9 November.

Batty, M. (1989) 'Enter a new arena for influence – inside Europe in the 90s', *Community Care*, 28 September.

Beagley, J. (1989) 'A place for migrants', *Social Work Today*, 5 October.

Behlmer, G. (1982) *Child Abuse and Moral Reform in England 1870–1908*, Stanford, CA, Stanford University Press.

Beresford, P. and Croft, S. (1986) *Whose Welfare?*, Brighton, Lewis Cohen Urban Studies Centre.

Beresford, P. and Croft, S. (1990) *From Paternalism to Participation: Involving People in Social Services*, London, Open Services Project.

Beresford, P. and Lister, R. (1991) 'P for poverty and partnership', *Guardian*, 17 July.

Berry, L. and Doyle, N. (1989) *Open to Complaints*, London, National Consumer Council.

Brauns, H. and Kramer, D. (eds) (1986) *Social Work Education in Europe*, Frankfurt, Deutsche Verein für Offentliche und Privat Fursorge.

Brauns, H. and Kramer, D. (1989) 'West Germany, the break up of consensus and the democratic threat', in Munday (1989).

Brewster, C. and Teague, P. (1989) *European Community Social Policy: Its Impact on the UK*, London, Institute of Personnel Management.

Briggs, A. (1961) 'The Welfare State in historical perspective', *European Archives of Sociology*, 11, pp. 221–58.

British Association for Social Workers (1980) *Clients are Fellow Citizens*, Birmingham, BASW.

CAF de Calvados (1988) *Rapport d'activité*, Centre Socio-Culturel de Lisieux Hauteville, CAF, CAEN.

Cannan, C. (1992) *Changing Families, Changing Welfare: Family Centres and the Welfare State*, Hemel Hempstead, Harvester Wheatsheaf.

Cannan, C. Coleman, R. and Lyons, K. (1990) *In Europe 2, Links and Exchanges*, London, CCETSW.

Cassegrain, D. (1990) 'Synthèse des Rapports des groupes de travail et de la table rondes', *La Revue Française de la Service Social*, 156, pp. 15–17.

Castles, S. (1984) *Here for Good; Western Europe's Ethnic Minorities*, London, Pluto Press.

Cecchini Report (1988) *The European Challenge: 1992, the Benefits of a Single Market*, Aldershot, Wildwood House.

CERIS (1990) *Information Booklet*, Strasbourg, USHS-CERIS.

Cigno, K. (1985) 'Neighbourhood work in health and social services', *British Journal of Social Work*, 15, pp. 173–186.

CNAF (1987–88) 'Le travail social des Caisses d'Allocations Familiales', *Dossiers CNAF*, No. 4, Paris.

Cocozza, L. (1989) *Social Work Training in the European Community*, Report for IFSW Liaison Committee for Social Workers in the EC Brussels, Commission of the EC.

Cohen, P. (1990a) 'Going Dutch', *Social Work Today*, 25 October.

Cohen, P. (1990b) 'Pioneer spirit', *Social Work Today*, 8 November.

Collins, M. (1990) 'A guaranteed minimum income in France?', *Social Policy and Administration*, 24(2) pp. 120–5.

Colton, M., Hellinckx, W., Bullock, R. and Van Den Bruel, B. (1991) 'Caring for troubled children in Flanders, the Netherlands and the UK', *British Journal of Social Work*, 21, pp. 381–92.

Commission of the EC (1987a) *A Journey through the EC*, Brussels, EC.

Commission of the EC (1987b) *The Community Combats Poverty*, Brussels, EC.

Commission of the EC (1988) *Social Europe: The Social Dimensions of the Internal Market*, Brussels, EC.

Commission of the EC (1989a) Communication from the Commission on Family Policies, Com 89 363, Brussels.

Commission of the EC (1989b) *ELISE: Employment and Insertion Profiles*, Brussels, EC.

Commission of the EC (1989c) *Medium Term Community Action Programme to Foster the Economic and Social Integration of the Least Privileged Groups*, Brussels, EC.

Commission of the EC (1989d) *The EC and Human Rights*, Brussels, EC.

Commission of the EC (1990a) *Communication on the Elderly: Proposal on Community Actions on the Elderly*

Commission of the EC (1990b) *Community Charter of the Fundamental Social Rights of Workers*, Brussels, EC.

Commission of the EC (1990c) *Draft Notice from the Commission to Member States laying Guidelines on NOW & HORIZON Initiatives*, Brussels, EC.

Commission of the EC (1990d) *ERASMUS Directory*, Brussels, EC.

Community Projects Foundation (1989) European Resolution passed on Community Development, April.

Connock, M. (1987) 'Helping les miserables', *New Society*, 24 July, pp. 14–15.

Coote, A., Harman, H. and Hewitt, P. (1990) *The Family Way: A New Approach to Policy-Making*, London, Institute of Public Policy Analysis.

Coote, N. (1989) 'Catholic Social Teaching' *Social Policy and Administration*, 23(2) pp. 150–60.

Council of Europe (1987) *'Proceedings of the Joint Meeting on Human Rights & Social Workers'*, Strasburg Council of Europe.

Council of Europe (1989) 'Self Help and Community Development in Towns', Report to Council of Europe, March, Strasburg.

Council of Europe (1991) *La Cooperation Européene dans le demain social et de la politique*, Council of Europe, 11 March.

CREW Reports (1990) 'New Programme for elderly proposed with budget', March/April 1990.

Davies, M. and Sale, A. (1989) *Child Protection in Europe*, London, NSPCC.

Deacon, B. and Szalai, J. (1991) *Strategies for Welfare, East and West*, Hemel Hempstead, Harvester Wheatsheaf.

Delors, J. (1985) Preface to Vandamme (1985).

Dennett, J., James, E., Room, G. and Watson, P. (1982) *Europe against Poverty: The European Poverty Programme 1975–80*, London, Bedford Square Press.

Department of Health (1989) *Caring for People: Community Care in the Next Decade and Beyond*, London, HMSO.

Dingle, A. (1989) *1992 and all that*, Euro-link Age.

Dorrie, K. (1989) *Informationsschrift der Paritätische WohlfahrtsVerband*, Frankfurt, TR.

DPWV (1990) *Parität*, Frankfurt, TR.

Eaton, L. (1990a) 'A place in the sun', *Social Work Today*, 6 August.

Eaton L. (1990b) 'High rise settlers', *Social Work Today*, 23 August.

Eaton L. (1990c) 'Spanish cocktail', *Social Work Today*, 16 August.

Eaton, L. (1990d) 'Suntrap', *Social Work Today*, 6 September.

Eaton, L. (1991) 'Olympian tasks', *Social Work Today*, 9 May.

EF News (1988) *Social Dialogue across Europe*, Dublin, EFILWC.

EF News (1989) *Social Cohesion and Mobility*, Dublin, EFILWC.

EFILWC (1988) *Locally Based Responses to Long Term Unemployment*, Workshop Report, Dublin, EFILWC.

EFILWC (1991) *Programme for Work for 1991–1992 and Beyond: New Opportunities for Action to Improve Living and Working Conditions in Europe*, Dublin, EFILWC.

Ely, P. and Stanley, C. (1990) *The French Alternative: Delinquency Prevention and Child Prevention in France*, London, NACRO.

Eurag *Eurag Information Booklet* (1991) Graz, European Federation for the Welfare of the Elderly.

Euromonitor (1990) 'The other 1992', *Directory of Social Change*, May.

Eurosocial Newsletter (1987) 'Conference of European Ministers Responsible for Social Affairs', 45, Vienna, European Centre for Social Welfare Training and Research.

Flamm, F. (1980) *The Social System and Welfare Work in the Federal Republic of Germany*, 2nd English ed.

Flora, P. (1985) 'On the history and current problems of the Welfare State', in N. Eisenstadt and O. Ahimeir (eds.), *The Welfare State and its Aftermath*, London, Croom Helm.

168 *Bibliography*

Flora, P. and Heidenheimer, A. (1984) *The Development of Welfare States in Europe and America*, New Brunswick, Transaction.

Flynn, D. (1989) 'Fortress Europe', *Inside Europe*, Community Care Supplement, 28 September.

Garrish, S. (1986) *Centralisation and Decentralisation in England and France*, University of Bristol, SAUS.

Gough, I. (1979) *The Political Economy of the Welfare State*, London, Macmillan.

Grossman, G. (1988) 'Social work in the school setting: a developing interprofessional task', *School Social Work Journal*, 12(2), pp. 84–92.

Guyard, M. (1988) 'Les travailleurs sociaux face au traitement du chômage', *Informations Sociales*, 8.

Hagen, E. and Jenson, J. (1988) 'Paradoxes and promises', in J. Jenson, Hagen, E. and Reddy, C. (eds.), *Feminization of the Labour Force: Paradoxes and Promises*, Cambridge, Polity.

Hallet, C. (1987) *Critical Issues in Participation*, London, Association of Community Workers.

Hämäläinen, J. (1989) 'Social pedagogy as a metatheory of Social Work Education' *International Social Work*, 32, pp. 117–128.

Hamburger, F. (1989) 'Armut in einer reichen Gesellschaft'. *Westdeutsche schulzeitung*, December.

Hantrais, L., Mangen, S. and O'Brien, M. (eds) (1990) *Caring and the Welfare State in the 1990s*, Birmingham, Cross-National Research Group.

Hargreaves, A. (1989) 'The Beur generation: integration or exclusion?', in J. Howarth and G. Ross (eds), *Contemporary France*, Vol. 3, London, Pinter.

Harris, R. (1990) 'Freedom of movement', *Community Care*, 20 September.

Hartman, H. (1984) 'West Germany, poverty and the family', in R. Walker, R. Lawson and P. Townsend, (eds), *Reponses to Poverty: Lessons from Europe*, London, Heinemann.

Hayward, B. (1990) *A Perspective for a Global Approach: The Social Action Programmes of the EC*, Paris, Interim Report to EC.

Hegar, R. L. (1989) 'The rights and status of children – international concerns', *International Social Work*, 32, 107–16.

Henderson, P. and Scott, T. (1988) 'Cogs in the machine', *Community Care*, 2 June.

Hillestad Thune, G. (1987) 'Human Rights in International Law', Council of Europe, *Proceedings of the Joint Meeting of Human Rights and Social Workers*, Strasburg, Council of Europe.

Hilton, I. (1990) 'Cloud Cuckooland', *The Independent*, 19 November.

Hockerts, H. G. (1981) 'German post-war social policies against the background of the Beveridge plan', in W. J. Mommsen (ed.), *The Emergence of the Welfare State in Britain and Germany*, London, Croom Helm.

Hooper, F. (1987) 'An advocate or a collaborator?', *Social Work Today*, 5 January.

Hooper, J. (1991) 'Moroccans take refuge in typically Spanish form of protest', *The Guardian*, 13 February.

Hoskyns, C. (1985) 'Women's equality and the European Community', *Feminist Review*, 20, pp. 71–88.

IRIS Network (1990) *Information Booklet*, Brussels, CREW.

Jarré, D. (1990) 'Eurocentric', *Insight*, 28 March.

Jarvis, M. (1990a) 'Have skills will travel', *Social Work Today*, 17 March.

Jarvis, M. (1990b) 'Housing: a crisis contained', *Social Work Today*, 12 April.

Jarvis, M. (1990c) 'A World apart', *Social Work Today*, 19 April.

Jones, C. (1979) 'Teaching social policy: some European perspectives', *Journal of Social Policy*, 8(4), pp. 509–26.

Jones, K. (1988) *Experience in Mental Health: Community Care and Social Policy*, London, Sage.

Jubineau, D. (1990) 'Assistants sociaux et RMI', *La Revue Française de Service Social*, pp. 5–8.

King, J. (1990a) 'An Olympic struggle', *Community Care*, 4 October.

King, J. (1990b) 'The poor relation', *Community Care*, 23 November.

King, M. (1988) *The French Experience: How to Make Social Crime Prevention Work*, London, NACRO.

Kosar, N. (1988) 'A psychosocial study of a group of young Turks living in the Federal Republic of Germany', *International Social Work*, 31.

Kosar, N. (1990) 'A world apart', *Social Work Today*, 19 April.

Lagrée, J. C. and Lew Fai, P. (1987) 'The 'insertion' of Youth', in Z. Ferge and S. M. Miller (eds), *The Dynamics of Deprivation*, Aldershot, Gower.

Lambrette, H. (1982) *Mutterfamilien und Vaterfamilien in Hessen*, Frankfurt, VAMV.

Léonard J. L. (1990) 'Le travail social à l'aune du RMI', *La Revue Française de Service Social*, 156, pp. 35–9 Paris.

Leaper, R. A. B. (1988) 'Cash and care in a European perspective', in S. Becker and S. Macpherson (eds), *Public Issues: Private Pain*, London, Insight.

Lippa, H. V. (1983) 'Interplay of public and private welfare in the Federal Republic of Germany', *International Social Work*, xxvi(2), pp. 1–8.

Lister, R. (1990) *The Exclusive Society: Citizenship and the Poor*, London, Child Poverty Action Group.

Lorenz, W. (1986) 'Social Work in Western Europe: themes & opportunities', in *Issues in Social Work Education*, 6(2), Sheffield, ATSWE.

Lorenz, W. (1991a) 'Social work practice in Europe – continuity in diversity', in M. Hill (ed.), *Social Work and the European Community*, London, Jessica Kingsley.

Lorenz, W. (1991b) 'The new German Children and Young People Act', *British Journal of Social Work*, 21(4), pp. 329–39.

Lunn, T. (1989) 'Inside Europe in the '90s', *Community Care*, 28 September.

Lunn, T. (1990) 'Public ends and private means', *Community Care*, 30 November.

Mangen, S. (1985) *Mental Health Care in the European Community*, London, Croom Helm.

Markopoulou, C. (1990) 'Social Services and Minority Groups in Greece', unpublished Ph D thesis, Sussex University.

Marsh, D. (1991) 'Brothers but strangers in their own land', *Financial Times*, 1 June.

Martinez-Brawley, E. (1991) 'Social services in rural Catalonia', *International Social Work*, 34(3), pp. 265–86.

Mayer Fabian, G. (1987) 'Social Assistance and social welfare services in the Caselaw of the European Social Charter', in Council of Europe, *Proceedings of the joint meeting on Human Rights and Social Workers*, Strasbourg.

McConnell, C. (1990) *A Citizens' Europe?*, London, CDF.

Mény, Y. (1987) 'The Socialist decentralisation', in G. Ross, S. Hoffman and S. Malzacher (eds), *The Mitterrand Experiment: Continuity and Change in Modern France*, Cambridge, Polity.

Merlo, J. (1990) 'RMI et insertion', *La Revue Française de Service Social*, 156, pp. 27–34.

Meyer, C. and Derrien, M. (1990) 'Maltraitance: Reflexions sur ce qu'en disent les médias', *La Revue Française de Service Social*, 156, pp. 44–5.

Mishra, R. (1981) *Society and Social Policy: Theories and Practice of Welfare*, 2nd edn, Basingstoke, Macmillan.

Meyer, P (1983) *The Child and the State*, Cambridge University Press.

Moss, P. (1988) 'Childcare and equality of opportunity', Report to the EC.

Munday, B. (ed.) (1989) *The Crisis in Welfare*, Hemel Hempstead, Harvester Wheatsheaf.

Munday, B. (1990) *Social Services in the EC, and the implications of 1992*, University of Kent.

Neate, P. (1990) 'Students talking shop', *Social Work Today*, 11 October.

Paillusson, M. T. (1990) 'Application du dispositif les ambiguités soulévées', *La Revue Français de Service Social*, 156, pp. 11–14.

Philpot, T. (1989) 'Bringing home the bacon', *Community Care*, 16 November.

Philpot, T. (1990) 'Bridge over troubled waters', *Community Care*, 27 November.

Pilkington, E. (1990) 'A safe haven?', *Education Guardian*, 20 November.

Prondzynski, I. (1989) 'The social situation and employment of migrant women in the European Community', *Policy and Politics*, 17(4), pp. 347–54.

Rapoport, R. (1989) 'Ideologies about family forms', in K. Boh, G. Sgritta and M. Sussman (eds), *Changing Patterns of European Family Life: A Comparative Analysis of 14 European Countries*, London, Routledge & Kegan Paul.

Redding, D. (1990) 'No (official) place to rest their heads', *Community Care*, 15, November.

Reive, G. (1987) *Community Care Services, An Overview*, Dublin NESC.

Resolution 208 (1989) 'Self Help and Community Development in Towns', Standing Conference on Local and Regional Authorities of Europe, 7–9 March.

Reynolds, S. (1988) 'The French Ministry of Women's Rights 1981–6: modernisation or marginalisation?', in J. Gaffney (ed.), *France and Modernisation*, Aldershot, Gower.

Richards, M. and Righton, P. (1979) *Social Work Education in Conflict*, NISW Paper 10, London.

Richardson, A. (1983) *Participation*, London, Routledge & Kegan Paul.

Rifflet, R. (1985) 'Evaluation of Community policy 1952–1982', in Vandamme (1985).

Rodgers, B., Doron, A. and Jones, M. (1979) *The Study of Social Policy: A Comparative Approach*, London, Allen & Unwin.

Rodrigues, F. (1990) 'Social work education, a view from Portugal', *Issues in Social Work Education*, 10 (1 & 2), pp. 156–69.

Rood-de Boer, M. (1984) 'State intervention in the family in the Netherlands', in M. Freeman (ed.), *State, Law and the Family*, London, Tavistock.

Room, G., Lawson, R. and Laczko, F. (1989) 'New poverty in the EC', *Policy and Politics*, 17(2), pp. 165–176.

Ross, G. (1987) 'From one left to another: 'le social' in Mitterrand's France', in G. Ross, Hoffman, S. and Malzacher, S. (eds), *The Mitterrand Experiment: Continuity and Change in modern France*, Cambridge, Polity.

Rossell, T. and Rimbau, C. (1989) 'Spain – Social Services in the post-Franco Democracy', in B. Munday, ed. (@). *The Crisis in Welfare*, London, Harvester Wheatsheaf.

Runnymede Trust (1987) *Combatting Racism in Europe: A Report to the EC*, London, Runnymede Trust.

Schiller, H. (1983) 'Current Situation and Trends in European Social Work Education' *International Social Work*, XXVI (3), pp. 1–6.

Schorr, A. (1965) *Social Security and Social Services in France*, Washington, DC, US Government Printing Office.

Scott, T. and Henderson, P. (1989) *The Circonscription system in French Social Services: Its Relevance to the UK*, London, NISW.

Seebohm Report (1968) *Report of the Commission on Local Authority and Allied Personal Social Services*, Cmnd 3703, London, HMSO.

Senioren-Charta (1990) International Tgung: Senioren fur ein Europa Frieden und Freiheit, 8 May, Bonn.

Sorenson, A. (1989) 'Women's economic vulnerability: the case of single mothers', Paper to EC Conference on Poverty, Marginalisation and Social Exclusion, Alghero.

Spicker, P. (1990) 'Solidarity', Paper to Social Policy Association Conference, University of Bath.

Spicker, P. (1991) 'Solidarity' in Room, G. (Ed.) *Towards a European Welfare State*, University of Bristol, SAUS.

Stathopoulos, P. (1991) 'Community development in rural areas of Greece', in M. Hill (ed.), *Social Work and the European Community*, London, Jessica Kingsley.

Stock, L. (1990) 'Schwerpunkt: Interessenveretung', LAG, 3 March.

Stone, K. (1990) 'Homage to Catalonia', *Community Care*, 20 September.

Stone, K. (1991) 'Learning to work together', *Community Care*, 19 October.

Textor, M. (1990) 'Helping multi problem families in West Germany: a new approach to social work', *Practice*, 4(1), pp. 56–62.

Thevenet, A. and Desigaux, J. (1985) *Les Travailleurs Sociaux (Que sais-je?)*, Paris, Press Universitaires de France.

Thomas, D., van Rees, W. and Swinnen, H. (1989) *Innovatory Training Unit*, London, NISW.

Townsend, P. (1990) 'And the Walls Came Tumbling Down', *Poverty*, no. 75.

Trades Union Congress (1988) *Maximising the Benefits; Minimising the Costs*, London, TUC.

VAMV (1989) *So schaffe ich es allein*, VAMV.

Vandamme, J. (1985) *New Dimensions in European Social Policy*, London, Croom Helm.

Wagner Report (1988) *Report of the Independent Review of Residential Care*, London, HMSO.

Wallace, H. (1990) 'Future of Europe: unfinished business', *Marxism Today*, December.

Wambst, A. (1990) 'Réflexion par trois professionelles', *La Revue Française de Service Social*, 156, pp 9–10.

Wedderburn, B. (1990) 'European Social Charter', *Association of University Teachers' Bulletin*, April.

Weghaus, B. (1990) 'Social assistance in the FRG', *International Social Work*, 33(4), pp. 365–73.

Which? (1991) 'Eurolaw and you', *Consumers Association*, June.

Whitting, G. and Quinn, J. (1989) 'Women and work: preparing for an independent future', *Policy and Politics*, 17(4), pp. 337–45.

Woodroofe, K. (1962) *From Charity to Social Work in England and the US*, London, Routledge & Kegan Paul.

Zapf, W. (1986) 'Development, structure and prospects of the German social state', in R. Rose and R. Shiratori (eds), *The Welfare State, East and West*, New York, Oxford University Press.

Index